LIFE

BARS

BRYAN HALL

BRIGHTON PUBLISHING LLC
435 N. HARRIS DRIVE
MESA, AZ 85203

Life Behind Bars

Bryan Hall

Brighton Publishing LLC
435 N. Harris Drive
Mesa, AZ 85203
www.BrightonPublishing.com

Copyright © 2013

ISBN 13: 978-1-62183-174-7
ISBN 10: 1-62183-174-4

Printed in the United States of America

First Edition

Cover Design: Tom Rodriguez

Photos: Mike Hill

DEDICATION

To Jennifer and Shannon; my biggest fans.
To Erin; who always encourages me.
To Mike; the best riding partner anyone could have.

Chapter One

An Idea

It all started with an idea…but then, most things do. The problem was, when I got to thinking, or I got an idea, especially about traveling, that idea gained a life of its own.

Even now, when I'm riding, or just looking at a map, I am constantly amazed that I can spend a day riding and end up two states away. I am very fortunate in the fact that, despite all the rainy weather I have to put up with in western Washington, within two hours of my house, I can be at the beach looking at the Pacific Ocean, or in the Cascade Mountains on Mt. Rainier, or at Mt. St. Helens—what's left of it, anyway.

I can be in the desert and wheat fields of eastern Washington, riding through the Columbia River Gorge east of Portland, or even crossing the border into Canada.

1

Long-distance riding is nothing new to me. I once did a trip from Olympia, Washington, to Missoula, Montana, and back—a little over 1,000 miles—in 22 hours. Likewise, a friend and I planned a couple of days on the road, and ended up returning home five days and 2,200 miles later. My friends and I would often ride 150 miles for lunch…just to be on the road and in the wind.

Two things played into my current idea:

First, ever since I was a young lad of about twelve or thirteen, I had wanted to go across the country. I didn't care how—bus, train, car, hitch-hiking, whatever. My desire was fueled by movies and television shows of people hitting the road: "Route 66," "Then Came Bronson," "Movin' On," "Two-Lane Blacktop," and such. Once I discovered motorcycles, there was no doubt in my mind. I was going to ride across the country.

And second, I love maps. I love looking to see where a particular road goes, or what surrounds a particular area. I would look at a map, see a small town and decide that's where I'm going. And off I would ride.

OK, so it took me only 40 years to do it. In all fairness, it's hard to do when you have a family, a mortgage—sometimes two—a job, and all the other crap that comes with being, or at least acting like, a responsible adult.

But, I digress. About three years ago, I was watching television, and the announcer was talking about

US Highway 50, which is often called "America's Highway," and "The Loneliest Road in America." Since Route 66 was only a shadow of its former self, Highway 50 seemed like a cool road to ride—right through the center of the US of A. And I thought, that's how I'm gonna go across the country. I called my friend, Mike, and told him about my idea. And, like many newborn things, the idea quickly got out of hand.

What started out as a plan to ride across the country in about two weeks or so, grew to include a return trip that expanded our timeframe to four, then five, then ultimately six weeks. Starting from the Puget Sound area of Washington, we would ride down the coasts of Oregon and California, head inland to Sacramento, and catch Highway 50 for the trip across the country to Ocean City, Maryland, 3,073 miles away.

Neither of us were fans of Interstate Freeways, so we decided that we would spend a couple of days in Washington, DC, head down across the Chesapeake Bay Bridge and tunnels, and then head home.

But, wait. The Blue Ridge Parkway was not too far from where we were going, so we added that to the list. And, once we got off the Blue Ridge, we were but a mere hop, skip, and a jump away from the Tail of the Dragon. More on that later—keep reading.

And, hell, we were back east already and, since we had to head north before we could head west, why not make it up to Cleveland and visit the Rock and Roll Hall of Fame?

Would ya looky there? Niagara Falls is damn near next door to Cleveland. Yeah, I know, not really, but on a map...Hey, how about if we forget about Chicago and head up the coastline of Michigan along Lake Huron, and over the Mackinac Straits? From there, we might as well just come across Highway 2 through Minnesota, Wisconsin, North Dakota, and Montana...and look...there's Glacier National Park.

Can you tell Mike and I were dangerous when we started talking road trips? We spent hours looking at maps, discussed possible routes, used reams of paper printing out directions and maps from Streets & Trips, and consumed just a few beers in the process.

The funny thing was, when it came down to it, we had a ride plan in place. But our attitude was, whatever happens, happens. Our plan was not carved in stone, and subject to—make that, destined to—change. We had no motel reservations, and the few people who had offered to put us up knew that we would call them the day before we got there. If we wanted to stay more than a day in a town, or if we wanted to ride more than we figured in a day, we would. And, if we felt we needed motel reservations, we could always call ahead from the road.

Since the trip, many people have asked how I packed for four or more weeks on the road, when all I had was two saddlebags. Not knowing what type of weather we would encounter, we had to take clothes and gear for most anything…well, except snow, since we did leave in July.

I planned on travelling light, and had a T-Bag and a pack on the back of the bike. One saddlebag was packed with gloves, extra sunglasses, one of my cameras—I took two—and other small items. The other bag was empty except for my tool kit. My strategy, after learning from other road trips, was that I wanted somewhere to stash my leathers and coat when the weather got warm.

I packed my medium-weight jacket, which was a denim jacket with a light liner and hood, my chaps, a sweatshirt, light, medium, and heavy-duty gloves, my raingear, two helmets, extra glasses, chargers for the cell phone and cameras, and my shaving kit. For clothes, it was enough for about four or five days, including socks, two pair of jeans, two t-shirts, and two tank tops. I did have a pack that attached to the back seat, which carried an extra gallon of fuel, a quart of oil, maps, papers, the extra helmet, and such. Mike packed much the same way, although he did bring along a laptop computer for us to use as well.

Some of the old-school bikers I know said I still packed too much. "All you need is some cash and a tool kit," they advised. But, while I believed in traveling light, I also believed in being prepared. That must be left over from the Boy Scouts or something.

People also asked how I was able to get that much time off from my job. Well, I had quit. I was working for a motorcycle dealer, and asking for six weeks off in the middle of the Pacific Northwest riding season was not really an option. But, truth be told, I was planning on a career change anyway, and this seemed like a good time to do it. Besides, everything else was in place—money, bills taken care of, future employment prospects, and a bike in great condition.

Of course, not being a complete idiot (*some will argue this point*) I did take steps to make sure my scoot was ready for the trip. I took it to my favorite bike shop and had them service it…anything to minimize the chance for breakdowns in the middle of nowhere.

This is a compilation of our trip across the United States and back. I'm not sure which one of us was Peter Fonda, and which was Dennis Hopper. But does it really matter?

CHAPTER TWO

OREGON COAST/NORTHERN CALIFORNIA

July 5

The big day was here. I loaded my scoot the night before, so I could just roll out of the garage and hit the road. The sun was shining, the clouds were few, white and fluffy, and the temperature was mild— perfect for heading out. There was almost nothing worse than taking off on a ride in the pouring rain, which was why we planned to leave on July 5. In the Pacific Northwest, the general consensus was that it didn't stop raining until the morning of the fifth.

I hit Mike's house in Olympia about 8:30 a.m. Our friend, Jessica, was there to take a couple of pictures. Then, off we went. We were hooking up with Mike's girlfriend at the time, Gig, just south of Olympia so she could ride with us to Seaside, Oregon.

We had a nice easy ride down I-5 to Longview, where we cut through town over to US 30 along the Oregon-Washington border. US 30 is a great ride for motorcycles, giving some nice views of the Columbia River and farmland, through the Coast Range past small towns, and into Astoria at the northwest corner of Oregon.

Oregon Border

The weather was warming up as we crossed the Young's Bay bridge between Astoria and Warrenton, and headed down US 101 toward Seaside. US 101 down the coast was a beautiful ride on a bike, one I have done numerous times, and one I have never gotten tired of. We stopped in Seaside for a quick snack, said goodbye to Gig, visited with my nephew for a bit, then headed south through Garibaldi, Tillamook, Lincoln City, and Depoe Bay.

We stopped a couple of times—once at the Tillamook Cheese factory, and then for a late lunch at a beachside restaurant in Depoe Bay called Tidal Raves, where we found good food, a nice simple menu, and fair prices. The restaurant sat on a bluff overlooking the Pacific Ocean, and the views were spectacular. Depoe Bay is known as the world's smallest harbor, and sits just off US 101. Waves running beneath the lava beds cause geysers to spout up to 60 feet in the air. And the bay itself is rich with many varieties of marine life.

From there we rode on through Newport and many little beach towns until we got to Florence, our stop for the night. The north coast was a much different landscape than the central and southern coast. It had sand and windblown trees on the north, and amazing rock formations along the southern coast. We were blessed with blue skies and mild temperatures as we made our way down the coast, except we got hit with the wind just south of Lincoln City that beat us up all the way to Florence.

Along the way, we hit a traffic jam. There was nothing moving, no cars coming the other way, and people were standing outside their cars. Yeah, like we were gonna sit there. After about five minutes of sitting, and noticing no other traffic coming from the other direction, we tooled up the wrong side of the road for about two miles, and passed cars, trucks, RVs, and other bikes until we could see the reason for the holdup.

Two cars had collided on a curve, and there were tow trucks and police everywhere. It was a good place to stop. We cut in front of a motor home, shut off the bikes and waited. A few minutes later, four of the bikes we had passed rolled up (*we're such trend-setters*) and jumped in behind us. The other bikers were also on a road trip, but they were from the East Coast. One was from New York, and one was from Ontario. After about a half hour or so, the road opened back up, and we were on our way.

We landed at a motel along the highway in Florence called the Villa West. It was a nice place. The owner, Conn, had bought the place a few years before, and was trying to get the word out that bikers were always welcome. They even gave us a couple of towels to wipe down the bikes in the morning.

The motel was an older motor-court style—our favorite kind—where we could park right in front of our room. Conn even had a couple of chairs to sit on out front of the room, which we took advantage of with some snacks and a drink or two of whiskey.

Since we'd had a late lunch, neither of us were really hip on rolling through town to find somewhere to eat, so I hoofed it across the street to a 7-11 and bought some crackers and summer sausage for dinner. Besides, we had clocked 360 miles since leaving home that morning, and a few drinks and watching the world go by was just what we needed.

We did learn something in Florence. Evidently, when one takes off from a red light—at least at the intersection next to the motel—it's customary to redline one's engine and/or burn off most of the tread from the rear tires on one's jacked-up, rusted '77 Chevy Blazer with burned-out mufflers. Note to self: Buy earplugs before the next motel.

July 6

Fog. This is what we in the Pacific Northwest call a marine layer—fancy speak for gloom. We wiped down the bikes, which turned out to be a recurring theme throughout our trip, and hit the road about 8:00 a.m.

The fog burned off rather quickly and, by the time we stopped in Coos Bay to visit the Harley dealer, the temperature had climbed to a comfortable level. But the wind was still beating us up. The highway on the southern coast toward Gold Beach turns away from the ocean and, once away from the wind, we could feel the temps rise about 15 degrees.

Of course, we managed to time our trip just right for the annual road construction and pilot car festival, so we spent some time sitting and waiting with many other vehicles. We stopped in Brookings for a quick snack about lunchtime, and crossed the Oregon-California border just after noon. Of course, that meant we had to grab a couple of pics at the state line. Some other travelers, from Germany, were happy to take our picture for us.

We got into Eureka about 3:30 p.m., and found a Motel 6. It was nothing fancy—hey, it's a Motel 6—but it offered decent prices and, again, we could park our scoots outside the room.

We had planned on staying in Eureka, as Mike had been telling me for years—and raving—about the Samoa Cookhouse. I was not excited. My twisted mind pictured fat guys in grass skirts, cooking Spam over an open fire, beating on drums and chanting. No, not that kind of Samoa.

The Samoa Cookhouse sat on the Samoa Peninsula just outside Eureka, and was part of an old logging camp. The cookhouse had been serving home-cooked food, and a lot of it, since 1890. According to the nearby museum, the cost for three meals per day for the loggers was 60 cents. All of the bread was baked in the cookhouse kitchen, and was served with butter from the company's dairy.

Owned at the time by the Hammond Lumber Company, the cookhouse operation was self-sufficient with only waste disposal and supplies coming from outside sources. Waitresses, who were required to be single and live in the upstairs dormitory, worked for $30 per month, which included room and board. They also had to work seven days a week for five weeks before earning a day off, which usually was on a Sunday.

The restaurant was the dining hall, and they serve family style—long tables with other people sitting next to you who you don't know. The menu was simple. What's written on the chalkboard as you walk in was what was being served. If you didn't like it, you could go somewhere else.

It was also all-you-can-eat. Our favorite kind of place. We rolled up about 5:30, went in, and sat down. The server brought us fresh homemade bread, with slices the size of a Buick, a tureen of soup, and a huge bowl of salad. The menu that night was pork steaks, pot roast, and baby carrots, baked potatoes, and dessert. The place wasn't real busy when we got there. But, while we were there, people began coming in. A bus full of blue-hairs on their way to Vegas filled the place up. By the time we left, it was packed.

Now, my experience with buffets and family-style restaurants had been that the food was marginal at best…usually bland and cold. Not so here. This place was amazing. The food was great, and always served hot. If you left hungry, it was your own damn fault. *(If you ever find yourself going to or through Eureka, California, make this place a priority.)* In fact, Mike and I may just take a weekend trip down there for the hell of it, just so we can eat there again.

July 7

Ah, nothing like a cold, damp, gloomy morning on the California coast. We hit McDonald's for breakfast. I'll tell ya now; when you're on the road and a quick, cheap breakfast is in order, Mickey D's is the place. I know guys who love to hit a sit-down restaurant, have a huge omelet or steak 'n' eggs, and then go riding. Yuk. I've never been one to eat a huge breakfast first thing in the morning, so a little something just to take the edge off, and get me through till lunch was all I needed. A Sausage McMuffin and a chocolate milk, about $2 (*I'm not a coffee guy*)…and I'd be good to go. And, even though we hit some mighty small towns along the way, there was almost always a Mickey's nearby.

OK, back to our story.

We rolled out of Eureka on US 101 under the infamous marine layer for about 30 miles until we saw the turnoff for the Avenue of the Giants. The Avenue of the Giants ran more or less parallel to the highway for 31 miles, crossing and running along the Eel River. It had more than 51,000 acres of redwood groves, and went through towns like Pepperwood, Redcrest, Weott, and Miranda. It then joined back up with US 101 just south of Phillipsville.

We were fortunate, we had hit the road early and, because of the time and the misty weather, we were pretty much the only ones on the road for quite awhile. More than a few times we were able to just stop in the middle of the road and get pictures of the trees, the wildlife, and the road itself as it wound through the forest. The views were amazing. I mean these trees were immense. Of course, we had to do the tourist thing and drive through a hollowed-out redwood to take our pictures—for the paltry sum of $4.

By the time we got back onto the highway, the sun had burned through the gloom, and it was warming up, which was fine with us. We sailed leisurely down US 101 about 100 miles, past Garberville and into Ukiah about 11:00 a.m.

Someone had gradually turned up the thermostat as we headed south, and it was topping 85 degrees when we hit town. We topped off the gas tanks, and grabbed a quickie bite at a Wendy's (*love those dollar menus*).We then stopped at the Harley dealer to find out what was the best way to get to Sacramento. By the best way, I meant the most-scenic, non-freeway route.

While we were at the Harley shop, we started to chat with a couple of folks who were waiting for their bike to come out of the service department. We discovered that they were from our area in Washington and, in fact, had been customers at the shop I recently had worked at. Small world.

Anyway, the parts guy, Jeff, told us to take Highway 20 out of Ukiah, and then turn onto Highway 16. He also mentioned we should stop just before Woodland at a bar he knew about called the Road Trip, that had good food and a biker-friendly atmosphere. Since Woodland was our intended destination for the night, we figured it would be a great place to stop.

What a remarkable ride—a mostly two-lane road with virtually no traffic. I think we saw maybe three or four cars in about twenty miles. We rolled through small towns and villages, past Clear Lake, around twists and turns just made for two wheels. Of course, all the while the temperature kept climbing and, by the time we turned onto Highway 16 and rode through Cache Creek Canyon, the mercury was topping 95.

After a few stops for water and shade, we cruised into the small town of Capay. And there, like an oasis, was the Road Trip Bar & Grill. Now, it didn't look real fancy on the outside, but what a great place. It was about three or so when we rolled up on the bar, so we thought it would be a fine idea to grab a cold beer or two.

The Road Trip was a building made up of a convenience store-deli, and the bar and grill attached to it. We walked into the bar, and saw that it was mostly empty—a couple of people at the bar, a bartender, a few people at tables, and stuff. Mike and I ordered up a pitcher, and talked to the bartender, Lila, a bit. This guy at the far end of the bar chimed in, and started asking about our trip—where we were from, where we were headed, what we were riding, and so on. He introduced himself as Jerry, and the lady next to him was Paula.

It turned out they own the place. They were friendly, righteous people—both riders. After crossing the country a few times, they had decided to open the Road Trip. Not only was the bar very clean, open and friendly, but Jerry and Paula had a huge picnic area out back with patios, tables, a stage, and a wall surrounding it all with Dave Mann-style murals painted on it. He told us they were always doing something with the community, like bike shows, bike nights, car shows, fundraisers, and such.

We were getting hungry and, with the temperature outside pushing the triple-digit mark, we opted to eat there rather than try to find a place in Woodland. Jerry said they made the best tri-tip steak sandwich around. So we ordered. And he was right. It was the best tri-tip I have ever had.

As much as we would have liked to have stayed for the night crowd, after about three hours we decided to get our lazy asses off the bar stools, and head down to Woodland to find a motel for the night.

It wasn't far. We cruised into Woodland about a half hour later, and found a motel—America's Best Value Inn. This would be the first of these motels we would stay in during the trip. The name fits the motels. It's nothing terribly fancy, but clean and reasonably priced. Plus, they had a rewards program" (*doesn't everyone now?*) that was different than most lodging chains. When you signed up, you got a card, and you got twenty percent off your room at check in. It was as simple as that. The one in Woodland was a nice, older, two-story motel, with parking right in front of the rooms—just our style. We unpacked, broke out the whiskey, and cranked the air conditioner.

July 8

This night found us in Dayton, Nevada (just outside of Carson City). Mike and I checked out of the motel in

Woodland, hit the road about 8 am, and took our time rolling toward Sacramento.

US Highway 50 starts in West Sacramento. We wanted to find the first road sign for this cross-country highway, and we did. In fact, it snuck up on us, and we had to turn around and come back to it. Highway 50 starts as part of Interstate 80's business loop, and we had plenty of room to pull onto the shoulder and grab the cameras. As we were taking various pics of the overhead sign and the roadside sign, suddenly we heard a voice over a public address speaker asking if we needed help. We looked around and noticed that a California Highway Patrol officer had pulled up behind our scoots. We told him we were fine, and he rolled off.

Mileage sign
Outside West Sacramento, California
The start of US-50

The roadside sign was really cool. It showed three destinations, and their respective distance: Placerville, 46 miles; South Lake Tahoe, 107 miles; and Ocean City, Maryland, 3,073 miles. Of course, we had to get photos of each of us in front of this sign.

We rode out of Sacramento, now on "America's Highway," and we sailed easily up into the mountains toward South Lake Tahoe. The weather was gorgeous— nice and warm, but not yet burning hot. The traffic thinned out considerably once we got away from the towns, and began climbing into the Eldorado National Forest east of Placerville.

Unbelievable scenery and views opened up to us as we carved through the twists and turns. We made a few stops for pictures, and to just drink in the views. At one point, we hit the 7,300-foot elevation mark, and could see Lake Tahoe off in the distance, bright blue and sparkling.

The closer we got to South Lake Tahoe, the more we could feel the breeze coming in off the lake, which kept the temperature down to a comfortable level. I had never been to South Lake Tahoe before, and I was expecting a little tourist burg at the end of the lake. I was wrong. The town was home to about 40,000 people, split between California and Nevada, and it had almost every store and shop you can think of.

The Nevada state line was right in the middle of town and, as soon as we crossed the intersection-state line, we saw casinos lining the street like sentries standing guard. Again, we made a few stops along the way for pictures of the lake and surrounding area, then it was off to Carson City for lunch, and a visit to the Harley shop.

At one point, we pulled off the road onto a gravel turnout for pictures of the scenic view, as we were still high enough to get a great shot of the valley below. Unfortunately, Mike's foot slipped and his bike went over on him, and into the gravel. I ran over, and helped him pick it up. While he was pissed, the only damage to the bike was the center console appliqué where he had his GPS mounted.

Oh, and, of course, his pride took a little hit too. Doesn't everyone's when that happens?

Once we rolled into town, we found our way to the Harley shop, and he picked up a new console insert. We hung out there for a bit, but it had kind of a weird vibe there. The place was not busy, even though it was a Friday afternoon, and the staff was not overly friendly. Well, the parts guy was, because Mike was buying something. They did have a meeting room-café-type of place there with vending machines and tables, so we grabbed a soda and hung out for a bit. We were planning to stay with an acquaintance of Mike's in Dayton for the night, and we had to hang out until she got home from work.

Anyway, we cruised on out of Carson City toward Dayton, about fifteen miles or so away. After checking the map, we found Dee Dee's house. But, since she was still at work, we headed back toward the main road, and found a little bar down the street to have a beer, and kill some time.

By the time we got back to Dee Dee's house, she was home, and we got settled in. Since she was kind enough to put up a couple of grubby bikers for overnight who she barely knew, we offered to take her out to dinner. Dayton had few places to eat other than the usual fast-food crap. We settled on the Gold Canyon Steak House, which was an old wooden house converted to a restaurant. We were seated right away, and our waiter, named Don, came over. This guy was probably the best waiter I had ever seen. He was funny, sarcastic (*which came in handy for a couple of smart-asses like us*), filled with stories and, most importantly, right on top of everything going on with his tables. Plus, the food was amazing. It was not overly expensive, but not bargain-priced either. It was worth every penny.

After dinner, we visited for a bit, and then hit the sack, as we wanted to be on the road by about 6:30 a.m. We came to find out a few months after returning from the trip, that Dee Dee had passed away from a form of cancer. We were, to say the least, very sad to hear it, as she was a very nice lady.

July 9

We were headed toward Ely, Nevada, about 350 miles away and straight across the high Nevada desert. This is called the "Loneliest Road in America," and for good reason. Once we passed through Fallon, and the Naval Air Station there, we were on our own until we reached Austin, just over 100 miles away. And, in those 111 miles or so, we counted a total of nine other vehicles on the road with us, and only one other motorcycle. Between Austin and Ely, about 150 miles, the road changed, and became curvier. More vegetation became visible as we climbed away from the desert floor. It wasn't much more crowded, however, as we still didn't see many vehicles.

While this was the loneliest road in America, and aptly named, it was nonetheless beautiful. Yes, it was high desert, but you could see for miles in any direction. And all along the roadway were these stone piles and stacks of rocks that were amazing. We climbed hills and dropped into valleys, and the temperature changed with every elevation change. Some of the passes we rolled over were as high as 7,500 feet, and the terrain seemed to change from sandy dunes and scrub vegetation to rocks and sandstone formations. Not since riding in Montana have I gone so many hours without seeing a house or barn.

US-50

Nevada

We made good time (*no traffic, duh!*) and hit Ely about 1:00 in the afternoon, with the temperature hovering in the mid-90s. Ely was an old mining town, that now makes a chunk of its money from gambling (*Nevada, you know*) and tourism. We checked into the Nevada Hotel on the main drag through town. The Nevada is an old six-story building. When it was built in 1927 it was the tallest building in Nevada, and the state's first fire-proof one, as well. Back then, rooms rented for $1.50 per night. Parking was on the street out front, but they do cater to bikers. They have cleaning supplies, so we were able to wipe the bikes down and get the bugs off. Even better, they had cameras and people keeping an eye on the bikes 24 hours a day.

We got checked in, had a small but comfortable room and the prices were still a bargain. We paid less than $40. We did the tourist thing, wandered through town a bit, stopped for a beer and a game of pool at a local tavern, roamed around the casino, and had our free drink at one of the casino bars. Then we had dinner in the casino. It was not bad either—a little diner kind of place with a lot of pictures of celebrities and stuff showing the history of the town and motel. Good steak.

July 10

We hit the road about 6:00 a.m., as we wanted to beat the heat, and we had planned a long day ahead of us—about 450 miles through Utah and into Colorado. US 50 joined up with Interstate 82 about one-third of the way through Utah and, according to the map, there was not much to see in this part of Utah. We had heard a possibility of thundershowers, but with the temperatures still hovering in the 90s, we weren't too worried about getting wet.

We stopped at McDonald's in Ely on our way out of town, and the counterperson had all the personality of a small soap dish. She clearly did not like her job. Nonetheless, the food was typical Mickey D's and hit the spot, without being too much for a long ride. As we crossed into Utah, the time zone changed and we lost an hour. But since we really had no schedule, it just didn't matter.

We topped off the tanks at the state line, and sailed leisurely through the curves, hills and valleys while stopping at almost every little town along the way to top off the tanks. The areas between towns were quite remote, and we had no desire to run out of gas in the middle of nowhere.

We rolled into a small town called Salina about 11 or so, and decided this would be as good a place as any to grab some lunch. Salina was where US 50 joined I-70 for the rest of the way to the Colorado state line. We could see some of the promised thunderheads in the distance, but skirted the first few as we headed out of town.

Mike's reflection in my mirror

Somewhere in Colorado

A short way out of town, we started dropping into the valley…down, down, down, we went until we saw the sign that said "Summit 7500 feet." I'm not sure how high we were before that. The next sign we saw was "Road

25

Slippery when Wet for 12 Miles," and, just as if on cue, the skies opened up.

They must know something in Utah that most people don't, because that was exactly how long it rained— twelve miles. And, suddenly, the rain stopped, the sun was out, and the road was bone dry—just as if we had gone through a doorway. There was no gradual lessening of the rain, no parting of the clouds, and no slow climb of the temperature. No, this was immediate and sudden. It almost gave us a "Twilight Zone" vibe.

Following the Interstate farther down in elevation, we came around a curve and over a small rise, and the landscape changed drastically. I could have sworn we were on the moon. We saw sandstone cliffs, towering rock monuments and views of a valley floor many miles below. Fortunately, there was a rest area/scenic viewpoint that we stopped at for pictures, and to explore some of these wind-carved rock formations.

The other thing we saw, looking out over the valleys, was an ominous, black, angry thunderstorm. We could hear the boom of the thunder emanating from it, and feel the electricity in the air from the lightning. As we were parked, we watched the storm advance toward us.

Hmmm. Time to go. We blasted back up onto the super slab, and we could see we were headed into another thunderstorm. We pulled over, dug out the raingear, and donned our rain jackets, as this one looked to be a soaker.

Murphy's Law was in effect that day, as we caught a few sprinkles, but it wasn't really even enough to get wet at 75 miles an hour. We skirted the edge of that cell, and outran the ominous black one that we saw from the rest area. As we dropped down toward the Colorado state line, we cleared the thunderstorms and, accordingly, the temperature climbed about 20 degrees. We were dying.

As we neared Colorado, we came to a small town called Green River, and stopped to shed the raingear and gas up. Next stop was the obligatory photo op at the "Welcome to Colorful Colorado" sign. There were stickers and graffiti all over this sign and, of course, being the fine citizen that I am, I added my own "hiwayflyer.com" to it with my Sharpie.

Grand Junction sits just about 35 miles inside Colorado at this point, and we decided to stop and grab a motel for the night. We found a great room at America's Best Value Inn for $52. It was a huge room, was close to restaurants, had a pool and hot tub, and the clerk was very helpful and friendly.

We got the bikes unpacked, cranked up the AC in the room, and headed off for dinner. So, evidently, here's the thing about Grand Junction, Colorado, on a Sunday— nothing was open. We saw a few restaurants within walking distance of the motel, but none were open on Sundays. Of course, the fast food joints were all up and running, but that was the last thing we wanted after a 400-plus-mile ride. A couple of blocks away we spied a Village

Inn, and figured that was our only choice for real food. Silly us. The food was bland and lukewarm, the service sucked, and the prices were too high for what we got. Oh well, can't have everything, I guess. After a short walk back to the motel, we poured a couple of whiskeys, and sat in the hot tub to loosen up the muscles a bit. Good day.

CHAPTER THREE

EAST OF THE ROCKIES

July 11

We got ready to leave Grand Junction, and discovered that the Harley dealer was right down the road from the motel. We rolled into the parking lot just as they opened. The sign in the parking lot said it was 8:58 a.m., and 84 degrees. Perfect riding weather.

This was a nice place, nice people, and they also sold BMWs and KTMs, and stuff. We picked up a couple of souvenirs, and hit the road, back onto US 50, and rolled up into the mountains to Montrose, about 50 miles away.

The temperature dropped as we climbed toward Montrose, and the clouds were thickening and getting heavier as we got closer. Since it was no longer 84 degrees out—it seemed like the temp had dropped to about 65—we put our long sleeves, coats and heavier gloves on.

The Weather Channel had talked about scattered rain and thunderstorms later in the day. I'm not sure what Coloradoans (*Coloradans? Coloradoites?*) call "later in the day," as this was still about 10:30 a.m. Anyway, we kicked the bikes into gear and climbed from 5,800 feet at Montrose to 7,700 feet, rolling along the Blue Mesa reservoir on the 155-mile ride into Gunnison.

We hit Gunnison, population 5,900, just about noon, gassed up, and grabbed a bite for lunch. Here's the funny thing we noticed about most of these small towns as we headed toward the middle of the country: There was always at least one fast-food joint in town, usually the obligatory Mickey Ds or Burger King, or often a Dairy Queen. As we rolled through Gunnison on US 50, the only fast food joint we saw was Sonic. And from that point on, most every little town, burg, village, city we rolled through had a Sonic. These things were everywhere.

Anyway, we grabbed a bite and watched the thunderstorm build…and build…and build. Thinking we could possibly outrun this one (*hey, I said "possibly"*), we headed off for Canon City, about 120 miles away over the Continental Divide at Monarch Pass, which was at 11,000 feet. Mike was leading and, about ten miles out of Gunnison, he pulled over. It was time for the rain gear, as the skies were just getting angry. We donned the chaps, rain gear, helmets, and gloves, and headed off into the rain.

We got up to the pass and stopped for pictures. This was amazing. The view, even though there were tons of clouds, was immense and breathtaking. We got sprinkled on a little bit, not like we had thought from the looks of the clouds, but I think we managed to skirt the worst of the rainstorm. We saddled back up and headed down the mountain toward Canon City.

Monarch Pass

Colorado

Canon City was a municipality of about 16,000 people, and was the seat of Fremont County, as well as its most populated city. It definitely had that small-town feel, except for the nine state prisons and four federal penitentiaries. Yes, folks, you read right—13 prisons in all.

The Colorado Department of Corrections operated the Colorado Territorial Correctional Facility, located in the town of Canon City. Then there were the Colorado State

Penitentiary, Arrowhead Correctional Facility, Fremont Correctional Facility, Skyline Correctional Center, Four Mile Correctional Center, and Centennial Correctional Facility all in the unincorporated area of Fremont County. Until mid-2009, the county also was home to the Colorado Women's Correctional Facility. The city straddled the Arkansas River, and was popular for whitewater rafting, fishing, rock climbing, and general sightseeing

As we dropped down the east side of the Rockies, someone turned the thermostat up. While it was roughly 60 at best on the pass, it was in the high 90s in Canon City. We shed the gear, gassed up, and noticed the thunderstorm rolling into town right behind us.

We beat feet out of town, and abandoned our original idea of getting to La Junta, which was still about 90 miles away. With the storm hot on our tails, bucking a kickass headwind, and another thunderstorm to the north, we opted instead for Pueblo, about a half hour away.

Once we hit Pueblo, we found a Motel 6 and pulled in. Yes, he had a room. Yes, we got a good price. Yes, we walked over to our room and opened the door. Yes, there was someone in the room—not the maid, not the maintenance guy, but someone sitting on the bed watching television. Oops.

We went back to the office, and told the kid behind the desk about it. He tried giving us another room, but the lock was broken. He offered to give us a suite—at a Motel 6?—for more money, and we said no, we'll take it for the same money. He, of course, could not do that without the manager, so we asked where the manager was. He told us he was on a conference call.

We waited.

Finally the manager came out, found out what was going on and, lo and behold, found us another room that had a lock and no one in it. There was a Howard Johnson's next door (*guess we should have stayed there...*) with a bar-restaurant called Visions, so we walked over there for a beer and some grub.

They had just built and opened the place, and were still in the process of setting it up. We talked to the bar manager—a really nice lady named Sophia—and had a few drinks. The bar menu was mostly finger food, typical appetizer-type stuff, but nothing that really grabbed our attention.

The bartender asked if we were going to eat. We said we really did not see anything that looked all that good. This caught Sophia's attention. She came over and asked what we wanted to eat—anything we wanted, and she would have the kitchen make for us. We mentioned we really didn't want anything too heavy, so she went back and had them make a couple of chicken Cobb salads for us. This was probably the best Cobb salad I had ever had, and it was only $6. We spent a good chunk of the evening there drinking far too many beers. We finally staggered back to the room, took a peek at the map for some idea of where we were headed the next day, and crashed for the night.

July 12

We were up and on the road early again. The thunderstorms had disappeared, and the weather gods were promising high temperatures again. Beautiful morning.

We gassed up, grabbed a quick bite, and headed out of town. About fifteen miles out of town, Mike flew past me and signaled for me to pull over. It seems his high-pressure fuel line had ruptured, and it was spraying fuel all over his left leg.

We took a peek at it. We saw the fuel line had been rubbing for a long time on the horn bracket, and it had finally rubbed through. So, it was time for a little roadside surgery. We wrapped the line in electrician's tape, knowing it wouldn't last long, but hopefully long enough to get to the next town. It lasted about 35 miles. Back on the side of the road again, I found an old Pepsi bottle in the ditch, sliced a section of it off, and wrapped it around the fuel line, with more tape and some zip ties.

Road surgery on Mike's bike

Colorado

Down the road we went, for about 75 miles until we got to this little town called Lamar, and saw that it was leaking again. This time, however, we pulled into an auto parts store parking lot, and I told Mike I had an idea. I went in and asked the counterman if they sold bulk fuel hose. They did. So I bought about six inches of fuel hose, and some more zip ties, and went back out to the bike. I sliced the hose lengthwise, and wrapped it around the leaking fuel line. I then wrapped it up with more tape, and zip tied the shit out of it. Success! No leak when he fired up the bike. Mike called the Harley dealer in Dodge City, Kansas (*nearest one to us at that point*), and told them what he needed. They said to come on in, they would fix him up. Sweet.

I had noticed, as we were working on the bike, that there was a motel across the street with a reader board out front. The reader board said, "American Owner." I told Mike I had to get a picture of that, and broke out the camera.

As we got ready to saddle up, I noticed a pickup pulling into the motel parking lot with another reader board in the back of it. This one said, "Holiday Motel. American Owned." After parking the truck, this little old guy got out and disappeared into the office. OK, this was too good to pass up. I trotted across the street, went into the office and asked if he was the American owner. He and his wife were sitting there watching television, and she said, "Yup. For seven years now." They were a cute couple.

I shook his hand, told him I thought that was awesome that he advertised that way. He was 84 years old, had bought the place when he was 77, and it was the only American-owned motel in town. Lamar had about 9,500 people in it, and roughly ten hotels and motels. We chatted for a while. He even showed us some of his rooms, which started at $37 a night. If we had ended up in Lamar in the late afternoon, instead of 10:00 in the morning, we would have stayed.

So, back on the road, we headed for Dodge City, about 150 miles away. We hit Dodge City about 2:00 p.m., crossed another time zone on the Kansas state line, and it was triple-digits hot and muggy.

We made our way to the Harley dealer (*edge of town with a gravel parking lot!*), parked, and went in to the service department. OK, this place looked like it should have said, "Harley-Davidson and International Harvester dealer." Anyway, Mike told the guy he was the one who called about the broken fuel line.

The guy behind the counter said, "Oh, yeah. Where's your fuel line?"

"Ummm. You guys have it, right?"

The dude then said he had thought that Mike had one.

Mike mentioned (*fairly nicely, given the circumstances*) that if we'd had the line, we would have put it on ourselves, and wouldn't have needed to be here.

They decided to do some checking, and found the only dealer in the state that had one was in Olathe, just outside of Kansas City, 325 miles away.

While we were hanging around the Harley dealer, one of the office workers came out and asked if we wanted some ice cream. It seemed that someone had brought in this huge ice cream cake, and they were trying to eat it before it melted—being as it was like 400 degrees outside, and all.

She sliced off a giant slab of cake and gave it to us to eat while we were waiting on the service guys to tell us they had found the part for Mike's scoot. After a few minutes, they told us they had made a quick phone call to the dealer, and they had asked them to hold the fuel line for us. So, off we went to find a motel.

Heading toward Kansas City was not a huge issue, as we were headed that way, and planned on staying there the next day anyway. But we didn't know if our latest road surgery would hold for another five-plus hours of riding in triple-digit heat. As it was, we found this little motel (*quick: guess what style of place it was!*) called the Holiday Motel, which had reasonably priced rooms and air conditioning.

We cranked up the A/C to frigid, washed some of the grime off our faces, and unpacked our scoots—except, the A/C was really not keeping up with the heat. But we thought we'd give it a chance, because lo and behold, there was a sports bar right across the street.

Mike and I jogged across the highway to grab a few cold, frosty libations, and talk about where we wanted to eat dinner. This place was pretty cool…and not just 'cuz of the air conditioning that they had going full blast. It was a pretty big place with a dozen or so pool tables, dart boards, video games and a bar that was busy. After a couple of brews, we decided to eat there, as the menu and the food looked pretty good.

Many beers, a few dollars thrown into the jukebox, (*Allman Brothers---great road music!*) some dinner, and more than a couple of games of pool later, we landed back in our room for the night. The A/C had cooled the room down a bit, but definitely was not working the way it should have. Oh well, it was good enough, as it was about 10:00 p.m., and the temperature outside had dropped to a bone-chilling 79 degrees. It didn't take long to fall asleep.

July 13-14

The next morning dawned bright and sunny, so we got on the road about 6:30 a.m., as the temps were already hitting the mid-70s, and we wanted to get to the Harley dealer in time for them to fix Mike's scoot.

It was a gorgeous morning in Kansas, with the sun coming into view behind the grain elevators on the edge of town, and no traffic on the road.

After gassing up, we blasted out of town on US 50, with Mike in the lead, and rolling easily along at about 75 miles an hour. Roughly twenty miles out of town, we passed a line of about three or four cars headed the other way. I thought one looked suspiciously like an unmarked police car—you know, generic color, Ford Crown Victoria, a few antennas on the trunk lid, plain hubcaps...the works.

About three or four minutes later, Mike started to pull over and I thought his fuel line had begun to leak again, but then I checked my mirror and saw the flashing blue lights. Yes, it was the Kansas State Patrol wanting to discuss the notion of our 75-mile-an-hour speed versus their 65-mile-an-hour posted speed limit. Oops. Hell, it's

Kansas. What do you need a speed limit for anyway? We pulled over, and up walked the trooper—all 5'7" of him and his large state trooper-issued hat. He informed us of the speed limit on that particular stretch of highway, and asked where we were headed, adding that he thought we were a long way from home.

We spent some time chatting about the trip, why we were blasting our way toward Kansas City, and how we were planning on heading back home. Officer Kansas was intrigued about us spending six weeks on the road—jealous, maybe?—and he even looked at our road repair on Mike's bike. He was impressed that it was holding up after being repaired on the side of the road.

He was truly a nice dude. Bottom line is, we got written warnings. And when Mike asked him how long it would take us to get to Kansas City, he replied, "Depends. You gonna do 75 or 65?" Let's just say we'll do 65. He told us we could figure on about three or four hours, and we headed off—at 65, for awhile. OK, it was a short while, but still…

We finally made it into Olathe without further incident, and found the Harley dealer, Rawhide Harley-Davidson, sitting just off the highway in plain sight. They were a great bunch of guys. They said they would get right on his bike since we were travelling. We wandered off to look around the store, scope out the new bikes, look at the cute sales girls, and buy a couple of souvenirs.

They took his bike back into the shop. I had them adjust my clutch, as it was feeling a bit tight. It wasn't too long of a wait, and a short while later we were ready to roll. We even got both of our bikes washed.

So, off we went to find a motel. We located another one of the America's Best Value Inns about seven miles or so from the dealer, so we wound our way through the city looking for it. About two blocks from the motel, at a stop sign, I hit the throttle and nothing happened. It was a broken throttle cable.

Sigh. I pushed the bike into a parking lot, called the Harley guys, and asked them to send a trailer. Sure enough, they picked up my scoot and took it back to the shop. Mike and I went to the motel, and checked in, had a drink and called the shop. Yeah, they didn't have the cables I needed in stock. Gotta order them.

Sigh. Let me explain. My scoot had a small set of ape hanger bars on it, which means the cables were about six inches longer than stock, in addition to being a braided cable, as opposed to the normal black vinyl.

Being that this was now late afternoon, they could not order the cables until the next day. And, if they could overnight them, we would be on our way on Friday.

Here's the good news. I had an extended warranty on my bike, so the cables, towing, labor were all covered. I did have to pay a small difference between the prices of the braided cables versus the stock ones, but it was minimal anyway. Even better, my motel and meals, since I was travelling, were covered too.

Speaking of meals, we had heard about Arthur Bryant's in Kansas City for barbecue, but everyone at the dealer's, and the guy at the motel, told us to go to Fiorella's Jack Stack Barbecue instead. They all said it's much better food and it's only a couple of miles away, as opposed to going into Kansas City twenty miles away.

A couple of hours later we headed off for Jack Stack's, and when we got there we noticed a line waiting to get in. I'm a fairly patient guy, but Mike is not, and when we saw the line(*long line…*), we decided there was no way we were waiting outside, in the heat and humidity (*which by now must have been pushing 157%*) for God knows how long, for some barbecue. Besides, as Mike likes to put it, we were so hungry our stomachs were beginning to think our throats had been cut.

We headed into the Red Robin next door, (*poor substitute, I know*) and got seated right away. First things first, we got a couple of ice-cold brews in front of us, and ordered. We had a nice leisurely dinner and, when we got up to leave about 45 minutes later, we noticed that a couple of the people who were waiting at Jack Stack's when we had got there were still waiting. We hatched a new plan. Let's come back for barbecue tomorrow—for lunch.

And, so we did. We took a late lunch, rolled up about 1:30 or so, and got seated right away. This place would have been worth the wait. It was the best barbecue I have ever had. The cornbread and coleslaw were all made on-site, not the pre-packaged crap that some places try to pawn off. Service was awesome, they didn't try to rush us, and the servers were right on top of refilling water glasses and clearing our dirty plates. Needless to say, we didn't need dinner that night, so we opted for snacks and refreshing adult beverages instead.

July 15

I got the phone call from the Harley shop the next day shortly after lunch time saying my bike was done. They were able to order the cables overnight from a supplier in Texas, and got them installed as soon as they hit the door. These guys were awesome, and really knew the meaning of customer service. As the one service guy put it, "We don't want to keep you off the road any longer than we have to." I liked his style. Even better, by the time they were able to tag my extended warranty for everything, my out-of-pocket was only $75.

By the time we got checked out of the motel, got to the shop and loaded up the bikes again, it was about 2:30 p.m., and hotter than hell. We had picked up this heat and humidity coming off the Rockies, and it was following us all the way to the East Coast.

We grabbed a quick bite, and rolled down the highway, not overly ambitious, but wanting to get some miles under us as we had been idle for two days. We needed some road time. We had planned to make it to a town about 70 miles away in Missouri called Knob

Knoster. I'm not kidding. Not that there was anything special about the town itself, but we couldn't resist staying in a town with that kind of name. I know. We're all still twelve years old inside.

As it was, we headed out of Olathe on I-435/US 50, crossed into Missouri, and were just zipping along happy as can be, when Mike suddenly pointed to his head and pulled over. Oh, shit, now what? Truth is, we had ridden about fifteen miles past the state line before we realized that Missouri had a helmet law. Oops. So, we pulled over and put the brain buckets on. Then we rolled down the freeway until Lees Summit, where US 50 splits off from the superslab once again. We got into Knob Knoster, and found that there really was not much there, and certainly no place we wanted to stay. Of course, we did get a picture in front of the sign.

So we saddled back up and headed east another twenty miles to Sedalia. Sedalia was a cool little town of about 21,000 people at the junction of US 50 and US 65. It was founded as a railroad town in 1860, and was the county seat for Pettis County. The Missouri State Fair had been held there since 1899. Mike and I found a great little motel about a mile off the highway just out of town called the Super 7. It was one of the older '50s-style motor court places we like. They were reasonably priced, usually very clean, even though they were older, and we could park right in front of our room. This one was no exception—clean, updated, and $40.

We washed the road grime off, got the bikes unpacked, and headed into town to find an ATM and some dinner. As we rolled through town, we saw a few mom-and-pop-type restaurants and cafes that looked interesting, until we passed Kehde's—pronounced "kay-dees"—Barbecue. The place looked like it once may have been an old A&W-type drive-in, but now it had a railroad dining car attached to it. Barbecue wasn't necessarily our first choice after just having eaten at Jack Stack's, but there was so much character in this place we couldn't resist.

Good choice. The food was fresh; the iced tea was truly iced; the sauce was flavorful without being too sweet, and eating in the dining car was wicked cool. In addition, we got to talking to some people at the table across the aisle from us. It turned out they were from Oregon. Small world.

CHAPTER FOUR

July 16

D o you remember our recurring theme of up early? This was no exception. We were up about 6:00, and started packing up. We had the television on to the weather Channel (*our favorite when we are on the road*) and the local forecast was mostly a repeat of what we had seen the past few days—sunny, hot, and humid. In fact, I took a picture of the television screen with the current conditions—6:29 a.m., 75 degrees, 94-percent humidity, 73-degree dew point. It meant, as we headed out, we not only had to dry our bikes, but we were in shirt sleeves riding in the fog. That's something that doesn't happen in the Pacific Northwest.

Highway 50 was very interesting through this part of the country. It was part two-lane road, part four-lane road, and then part Interstate. And, even though the map seemed to indicate that 50 would take us right through St. Louis, as we got close we saw a turnoff for US 50 that dragged us through some neighborhoods and suburbs—strip mall hell.

Then we saw the White Castle.

I had never eaten at a White Castle before, so we had to stop. We grabbed some burgers (*I don't care that it was only 10 a.m.*), took some pics, sent a text to my girlfriend telling her that Harold and Kumar said hi. Then off we went again, and crossed the Mississippi River into Illinois. It's a good thing we don't have White Castles in Washington, or I'd probably weigh 400 pounds.

As we rolled through Lebanon, Illinois, we noticed a sign for "Old US 50." So, of course we took it. Old US 50 ran pretty much parallel to the current US 50, but went through some cool little towns like Trenton, Breese, and Beckmeyer, and a lot of farmland and corn fields for about 25 miles until the town of Carlyle, on the Carlyle Reservoir.

"Old US-50"

Outside Lebanon, Illinois

The reservoir is the largest man-made lake in Illinois, and was created due to a dam across the Kaskaskia River in 1958. As workers built the dam and the resulting 26,000-acre lake, they capped 69 oil wells, and exhumed 600 graves from seven small cemeteries. Construction of the dam started late in 1958, and the lake itself was dedicated in 1967.

We rolled through more farmland into Olney, and found another old motor court style of motel on the edge of town—old being the operative word. This place was probably built in the 1940s, and last updated in the 1980s. It was not as nice as the one in Sedalia, but it had air conditioning, and television. And we got a two-room suite with a full kitchen for $45.

Our room was tucked into a corner away from the street, and was actually pretty comfortable for being as old as it was. It sounds nicer than it was, but it was clean, quiet and close to restaurants.

After we unpacked and cooled off a bit, we saddled back up and headed for the local liquor store, and to explore the small town for dinner choices. The liquor laws here seemed weird to us. We couldn't buy beer, wine or liquor in the normal stores, only liquor stores. But, the liquor stores were all independently owned and operated. A converted gas station close to the motel was the one we chose, and we grabbed a six-pack, and restocked our supply of Crown Royal for the road.

Dinner that night was at the Elks Lodge. Yeah, I know. But, this place had a nice restaurant that was open to the public and killer prices for a rib eye steak dinner with all the goodies to go with it. And it was yummy.

One thing Mike and I had noticed as we checked into these small motels along our route was that many of them seemed to be owned and/or run by East Indians, and they all were named Patel. It turned out, when we looked it up one night, that Patel was basically the Indian equivalent of Smith or Jones. In fact, as of the 2000 US Census, Patel was ranked 174th among the 500 most common last names in the United States.

We even found numerous articles written about the Patel motel phenomenon. In the 1960s and '70s, a large number of Indian immigrants came to the United States with the intent of pursuing university education. Once they graduated, however, the MBAs and engineering degrees did not help them find jobs that paid well. A majority of them saved up while working blue-collar jobs, and then bought under-valued or run-down properties, and turned them into viable businesses. It is now estimated that as many as 60 percent of hotel and motel properties in the United States are owned by people of Indian origin, And one-third of these have the last name Patel. We must have stayed at most of them.

And that's your history lesson for the day.

July 17

Another early morning.

Now, understand that neither of us were really late sleepers anyway but, as I have said, the heat and humidity were doggedly following us across the country. Today was going to be no exception.

Plus, the weather people were talking about more thunderstorms. I love thunderstorms. I just don't want to ride in them—especially in the Midwest. They have a tendency to grow 'em big out there.

So, anyway, we got the scoots packed. Then we saddled up, hit the gas station, and rolled out of Olney by about 6:30 a.m., after hitting our old standby, Mickey Ds, for breakfast. We again had to wipe down the bikes due to the humidity and moisture in the air. We jumped back on US 50 and headed toward Indiana, about 35 miles east. We crossed the Wabash River on the Red Skelton Memorial Bridge and, not only were we in Indiana, we were also now in the Eastern Time Zone.

The good thing was, the temps were in the mid-70s, so it was a beautiful day of riding.

We rode through Seymour, Indiana, the home of singer John Mellencamp. Being a big fan of his, I was hoping to see where he grew up. Funny thing was, I didn't see any signs announcing it as such. Oh, well.

We made a stop for gas in Versailles, and it was my turn to have my pride hurt. I filled the tank, then went to park my scoot, and didn't get the kickstand all the way down. I leaned the bike over...and over...and over. Crap. Mike came running over, and helped me pick it up. There was no damage, as it went over slowly and came to rest on the engine guard.

Anyway, from Versailles, we rolled the rest of the way across the great state of Indiana, again detouring onto Old Highway 50 at Dillsboro.

As we cruised into Aurora, Indiana, we saw the Ohio River. Across the river was the State of Kentucky. Staying on US 50, however, as we did, took us up through Lawrenceburg, across I-275, and into Ohio. We then followed the river down through North Bend and Riverside, and skirted the south end of Cincinnati, where US 50 joined up with I-71 for a couple of miles.

About six miles east of Cincinnati, US 50 ran northward away from the river and ran toward Milford, then curved south and east. We followed it through a number of small towns and farmland (*great scenery*) until we got to Hillsboro, about 280 miles from Olney.

On the far side of town, we again found a cool little motor court motel, called the Greystone, for $40 a night. We did the usual tasks—unpack, wash the grime off, crank up the AC.

We had a really weird thing happen. I mentioned that we carried cameras with us, and each of us had pocket digital cameras that we could operate with one hand, and snap pictures as we were riding. Yeah, I know, not the safest thing to do…but, whatever.

Mike was clicking some pics as we skirted the south end of Cincinnati along the river. When we got to the motel (*no stops in between),* and unpacked the bikes, Mike's little camera was nowhere to be found. We searched his luggage, saddlebags, Tour Pak and all around the motel parking lot, but to no avail. We even thoroughly searched our room in case it had dropped unnoticed when we packed everything in. No luck. It was gone, never to be seen again. To this day, we have no idea where that little camera disappeared to.

When we checked in, the proprietor of the motel—Mr. Patel—told us there were a few restaurants in town. So, after resting up a bit and cooling off, we headed west into Hillsboro.

I don't know where all these restaurants were that we were told about. We saw Dairy Queen, McDonalds, Wendy's, Burger King, and others, but never saw any hometown type of places. The motel owner had told us there was a steakhouse in town as well. He said to turn right at the stop light, and it's down a few blocks. We couldn't find it either.

We discovered later on that he evidently did not know his right from his left because, if we had turned left at the stop, we would have found it. Oh well. We did see a little barbecue place (*gettin' tired of BBQ now*) and figured it was as good as any we'd seen.

Boy, were we wrong. We parked the scoots out front, and walked in. *Uh-oh, we're the only ones in the place.* First red flag. The owner was sitting at a table reading the paper. A young girl (*his daughter?*) seemed like we were really imposing on her peace and quiet, and told us to sit anywhere. I think we should have chosen to sit at the Wendy's next door.

Anyway, we ordered, and when the seriously overpriced food came, we both agreed it was probably the worst barbecue we had ever had, and quite possibly the worst meal in general we had had to date. The meat had no flavor, and was dry and tough. The beans came out of a can, and the coleslaw was some premix crap from a food service company. We paid, and left after eating maybe half of it. It was a good thing the girl didn't ask us how it was.

Anyway, we headed back to the motel for the night, but not until we made a stop at the local Dairy Queen for a cone.

July 18-19

We woke to another foggy 73-degree morning. This time it was so bad Mike and I could barely see each other. Even though it was 73 degrees, the fog kept a chill on us, and we were wearing jackets and sweatshirts.

About 120 miles into the day, we crossed the river into West Virginia, and made our way to Parkersburg for a gas stop and rest. The fog had lifted about an hour before, and we were once again comfortable in the mid-80-degree temperature. Once we left the industrial areas near the river, and the town of Parkersburg itself, the ride through the countryside was gorgeous. Rolling hills, nice twists and turns on the highway, and some absolutely beautiful views.

We stopped at a little mom-and-pop burger joint for lunch in Grafton, about 100 miles from the state line.

Once we saddled back up, we rode through more twisties and hills, and skipped through about eleven miles of Maryland, and then back into West Virginia. At this point, it was the most scenic ride we had taken on the trip. It's not that the desert wasn't beautiful, but this was amazing—lush green fields, farms, winding country lanes. You get the idea.

We found a motel in Keyser, a little town of about 5,500 people next to the Potomac River. One of the first things we saw in town was a Wal-Mart. Mike needed a new camera and a pair of sunglasses, so we stopped in. He bought and paid for the camera in the electronics department. Then we stopped at the optical center at the front of the store on the way out, where he picked up a cheap pair of shades. Here's the weird thing. It took about two days for the camera purchase to hit his bank account (*debit cards, you know*), but the sunglasses purchase never showed up. Gotta love free shit from Wally world.

Anyway, back to the story. Keyser is the county seat of Mineral County, as well as the home of Potomac State College, a feeder college of West Virginia University. When we asked the desk clerk about places to eat, she mentioned a few, mostly the chain and fast food places. But then she said something about Clancy's Irish Pub.

Irish pub? She had our attention. She told us where to find it, and off we went. What she didn't tell us was that they had moved. We found the old pub located in a dilapidated building downtown, with a sheet of paper taped to the window saying they had moved, and the address of the new place. It didn't take long, and we found it. Of course, we were a little worried about the ambulance parked out front.

Nevertheless, we went in, sat down, and the server came over to take our drink order. I'll say it right now: I am a beer snob. I like craft beers, dark beers, imported beers— beers I can chew. And one of my favorites, especially in an authentic Irish pub, was a Black and Tan, which was Bass

Ale with Guinness Stout poured on top over a spoon to keep the two colored brews separate. So, I asked for one. In English.

From the look on her face, I may just as well have asked her to chop off my little toe with a dull knife. And then she asked, "In a bottle?"

It seems that there was a brewery back east that made a Black and Tan in a bottle. Not Guinness and not Bass.

I told her no, and explained what a true Black and Tan was. She went away for a minute, came back, and said, "We don't have that."

Hmmm. Guinness on tap? Nope.

OK, whiskey and coke it is.

She left the menus, and told us their daily special for the day was wings—chicken wings. In an Irish Pub.

OK, it was West Virginia, and a bar, so I gave them that one. Mike ordered bangers and mash. I ordered shepherd's pie.

She delivered the food way too quickly, and Mike's bangers were basically two polish dogs sitting on top of some very dried-out looking potatoes that looked to be instant potatoes, with—are you ready for this?—sauerkraut on the side.

Then she put my shepherd's pie in front of me. At least, I think it was shepherd's pie. It was hard to tell, as it was buried under about two pounds of melted cheese. Well, some places will do some things a little differently. And cheese on top of shepherd's pie, while not true Irish fare, was not unheard of.

I cut into it with my fork, and saw the meat (*good*), potatoes (*again, instant*), peas (*yep*), carrots (*passable*), onions (*of course*), green beans (*what?*), corn (*huh?*), and Lima beans (*WTF?*). I think their idea of shepherd's pie was to dump a bag of mixed veggies in it, bury it all under some fake potatoes and cheese, and call it good. Oh yeah, they nuked it too, and their microwave must have been on its last legs, because some of my dinner was hot, but most of it was cold, not to mention tasteless and dry.

Because we were hungry, we ate it. Then we spent the rest of the night laughing about it, but mostly at ourselves. After all, we went to an Irish pub in West Virginia. What the hell did we really expect?

We were in no hurry to roll out of the motel in the morning. We had been on the road early almost every morning since Nevada, and we had planned only about a 180-mile day, since we were ending up at a friend's place in Annapolis.

When we did get up, and opened the curtains, we saw…rain. Our bikes were soaked. And, while it was not a downpour, it was steady. Of course, we clicked the television on to the Weather Channel, and saw the storm was passing through. By the time we wolfed down the free breakfast the motel offered, the rain had moved along nicely.

Mike and I got the bikes dried off and packed, and we lit out for Washington, DC, and Annapolis about 9:30 or so. Humidity was high, temps were about 75 degrees and, as wet as we were from the humidity, the wind cooled us off nicely as we rode.

The day wore on. We cruised leisurely through the Virginia countryside, and the thermometer kept climbing, along with the humidity.

Riding through Virginia on US 50 was amazing. It was gorgeous countryside and, since it rolls through Fairfax County, we saw huge horse farms and old homes with mile-long driveways.

Fairfax County is the most populated area in both Virginia and the Washington, DC, metro area. In fact, some say the population of Fairfax County exceeded the population of seven states. It also has the highest median income in the nation, and more than 50 percent of the adult residents have four-year, or more, college degrees. Gotta love government employment.

Mike and I have a very weird, and sometimes cynical, sense of humor, and it seemed like every day we saw something that made us laugh.

Case in point: Food trucks, and especially taco trucks, are a huge fad right now, at least in the Northwest. We saw a few here and there as we traipsed across the country. But, motoring down US 50 in one of the most expensive counties in the country, we saw a taco truck. Oh, but wait, this wasn't a regular taco truck. Oh, no. This one had "Spanish Food," according to the sign. You know, Spanish food, like tacos, burritos, and empanadas. Yeah, that's what we said. Snobbery was alive and well.

US 50 merged into I-66 to traverse the Theodore Roosevelt Memorial Bridge over the Potomac Rover, and into DC. The Interstate highway then split and headed north, while US 50 continued into DC proper. As it crossed 23rd Street NW, US 50 became Constitution Avenue, and ran along the National Mall past the Jefferson Memorial, the Ellipse, and the Museum of Natural History. It then turned left at the National Gallery of Art, and headed north across Pennsylvania Avenue. A few blocks further up, US 50 turned right and became the John Hanson Highway all the way into Annapolis.

Our plan was to get into Annapolis, get settled in with our friend, Gary, then head into DC on the Metro the next day. Of course, riding through DC was a challenge and, yes, we made a wrong turn (*or no turn when we should have*), and had to pull over to dig out the map. OK, now that we knew where we had to go to get the hell out of town, we made an illegal turn or two (*sshhh...don't tell anyone*) and made it back onto US 50, also known as the Hanson Highway.

The stretch of US 50 between DC and Annapolis was named for John Hanson, a public official from

Maryland during the Revolution. He was elected as a delegate to the Continental Congress in 1779, and was also a signer of the Articles of Confederation in 1781. That same year he was elected president of the Continental Congress, causing some biographers in 1898, and again in 1932, to put forth the idea that he was actually the first president of the United States.

After he served his one-year term as president of the congress, he retired from public office, and died in 1783 at his nephew's plantation. Hanson owned about 223 acres of land, and had eleven slaves at the time of his death. In addition to the section of US 50 named after him, Hanson also was featured on a six-cent post card in the 1970s, as well as a twenty-cent postage stamp in 1981.

Riding out of DC on the Hanson Highway, the muggy heat was almost unbearable. The moisture in the air had long ago stopped cooling us down. It was more like riding in a sauna. Where Mike and I live, riding on a hot day can still cool you down some, as the breeze feels cool. Not so here. It was like riding with a blow dryer on full blast aimed at our faces.

In addition, the clouds were building in the late afternoon heat, and we were beginning to wonder if we were going to get soaked. We made our way to Gary's, got the gear off our scoots, and went inside. Gary's place sat right on Chesapeake Bay near a yacht club. And, not fifteen minutes after getting in, the skies opened up with a vengeance. Thunder boomed all around us, lightning struck the water in the channel, and rain came down in torrents.

We had a great night hanging out and visiting with Gary. And, once we retired for the night, we were out.

CHAPTER FIVE

THE WHOLE TOURIST THING
July 20-21

Today was tourist day. We went into DC to wander around and look at the sights. The Metro commuter train did not come all the way to Annapolis, so Mike and I rode up to the park and ride at the end of the line and caught the train into DC.

Muggy. Muggy. Muggy. And hot, hot, hot. The heat was not so bad. The humidity killed us.

We wandered the National Mall, and made our way to the various memorials and monuments. I had been to DC twice before and, the last time I was there, the Washington Monument was closed for repairs. So, obviously, this time I wanted to go up. As luck would have it (*or just the National Park Service's way of doing things*), we could not.

If you wanted to go up in the Monument, you had to be there at something like 7:00 a.m. to wait in line for a free ticket, even though the Monument itself didn't open until 9:00. We found out that you could make a reservation for a free ticket, which would cost you $1.50 (*hey, it's the government*) but those reservations are limited and usually booked for months ahead of time. Shortly after we were there, about four weeks later, an earthquake damaged the Monument and the Park Service closed it until further notice.

We wandered through the heat some more, and found ourselves at the Vietnam Veterans Memorial Wall. Mike was looking for a name that he knew, and the volunteer guides there were extremely helpful and knowledgeable. The volunteers were there to help visitors find names on the wall, answer questions, and even trace the names of people engraved on the Wall. There were over 58,000 names listed on the memorial, and some visitors brought items to leave at the site. We found out from one of the volunteers that these items, if they are non-perishable, are gathered by the park staff and archived in a storage facility. The volunteer also told us that these archives are not open to the public. Names on the wall are arranged chronologically according to the date of the casualty. Directories that list the names of those on the wall are also available to help visitors locate the name they were looking for.

Of all the displays and monuments in the Mall area, this was by far the most emotional for both of us. It was probably because we are old—but more likely because the Vietnam War was a huge deal to both of us growing up. And, Mike had served over there.

Once he had found the name he was looking for, we wandered over to the Lincoln Memorial, and hid in the shade for a bit. We were a bit disappointed, though, as the Lincoln Memorial reflecting pool was empty, and undergoing a huge renovation project. It seemed that the pool was leaking. The government contracted the job out to replace the concrete pool on new pilings, to install a new system of drawing water in from the tidal basin instead of from the city water sources, and to install new lights, sidewalks, and benches—something like $31 million worth.

We hiked our way back to the Metro station, and past the White House. There were tons of Homeland Security dudes and vehicles hanging around, and I thought about waving to the Secret Service sniper on the roof, but thought better of it. Which brings up a point: Why are they called the Secret Service? They are not secretive at all. In fact, they stand out like a redneck at an opera. Just wondering.

Another one of those *"WTF"* moments happened as we were walking back to the Metro Station. We crossed a small plaza loaded with restaurants and cafes, and saw a banner-type sign that advertised a Cornhole League, sponsored by United Social Sports. Like I said, we're all twelve years old, right? We later found out (*from Gary*) that cornhole was a game like the carnivals had where you throw a beanbag at a board with holes in it and see how many points you can get. Who knew? It's not the definition of cornhole I had grown up with.

Anyway, enough of my ramblings. By the time we caught the train back to our bikes, we were soaked from the humidity, and the AC on the train felt really good. We hit Gary's after the short ride from the park and ride, and Gary announced he was taking us to eat in town.

We went to a place called the Davis Pub, which was a little neighborhood bar tucked away on a side street. It was packed. The place started out in the 1920s as a general store, and in the '40s became a lounge. It officially became the Davis Pub in 1986. There was outdoor seating, but no empty spots at all, and it looked like standing-room only inside as well.

We all went in to grab a beer, and Gary was talking to one of the employees. About five minutes later, they led us to a table in the back that was available. Their special that night was meatloaf (*one of my all-time favorite meals*), and after the disastrous meals Mike and I had eaten on the road the past few days, we were eager for some good food. We were not disappointed. We had huge slabs of homemade meatloaf, mashed potatoes (*real potatoes even!*) and gravy, and veggies—all for $9. We damn near couldn't finish it all. Around Annapolis, the Davis Pub is well-known as the neighborhood hangout, and it's easy to see why.

Mike and I headed back into DC the next morning, after Gary had taken us out for breakfast. He had been telling us how he wanted to take us to Chicken Ruth's while we were staying in Annapolis, and I was wondering what the hell kind of place we were going to. Currently owned by Ted and Beth Levitt, and stuffed into an old building downtown, Chick and Ruth's Delly (*"Chick and Ruth's"...duh*), along with the Scotlaur Inn, sits on the site of the original Annapolis City Hotel in a building dating back to 1899.

The Levitt family, starting with Chick and his wife Ruth, had operated the restaurant and inn in the Annapolis Historic District longer than any other. The original "deli" had a small rooming house upstairs, with twelve rooms and two bathrooms. Chick and Ruth had always wanted to establish a bed and breakfast Inn, but never had the resources. In 1986, however, a fire in the rooming house changed all that. Chick and his son, Ted, rebuilt and remodeled the entire upstairs to the current Scotlaur Inn Bed & Breakfast.

Ted grew up working the family business, and graduated from the Culinary Institute of America. He is at the business six and seven days a week, and up to fifteen hours a day. And every day one can find Ted moving like a whirlwind through the place, greeting customers, working the grill, taking customers' orders, helping the guests at the inn check in and out, and more.

He even came and sat with us for a bit as we ate. He told us about the restaurant, his love of antique cars, and his charity work with rider's groups all over the area. They served killer homemade food, and had a lot of regulars sitting at the counter. At 8:30 a.m. every weekday, and 9:30 a.m. on the weekends, everything stops, and everyone says the Pledge of Allegiance.

They even do man vs. food challenges, including a 6-pound milkshake, a 3-pound sandwich, a 3-pound cheeseburger, and more. Again, I'm not a huge breakfast eater, but when there is a good one, I'm all in. And this was probably the best breakfast I'd had in years. There is nothing institutional about the food here. It's all fresh, huge portions, mostly local, and cooked to perfection. Chick and Ruth's is a must-visit for anyone in the Annapolis area. Hell, it's almost worth a ride back just to have breakfast.

After stuffing ourselves at breakfast, we headed off for Arlington National Cemetery. Again, we rode to the park and ride, and caught the train into DC. Again, it was hot and muggy. It was only a short walk to the cemetery from the Metro station, and we roamed around the exhibits and visitor's center inside Arlington.

I had seen pictures and television shows about Arlington many times over the years, but nothing could have prepared me for the sheer size of it, and seeing all the headstones lined up in rows for what seemed like miles. Of course we made our way to President John F. Kennedy's grave with the eternal flame burning, and his family members buried nearby.

We also visited the Tomb of the Unknown Soldier. As we got to the latter, we noticed a crowd had gathered, and it was time for the changing of the guard. I grabbed my camera, and made my way through the people so I could get a vantage point for some pictures. It was inspiring, to say the least.

Changing of the guard

Tomb of the Unknown Soldier

Guard changes take place every 30 minutes, 24 hours a day, 365 days a year, and are strictly regimented. The guard takes 21 steps during his walk across the tomb, in reference to the 21-gun salute—the highest honor given to any military dignitary. At the end of his walk, he performs an about-face and waits 21 seconds, then begins his walk back across the tomb. His rifle is carried always on the shoulder away from the tomb, and his gloves are wet to keep from losing his grip on his weapon.

All this took place in almost triple-digit temperature, with humidity in the 90-plus-percent range, in full dress uniforms.

We further learned that the guards must meet very strict physical characteristics, and must commit to serving two years to guard the tomb. They live in a barracks under the tomb for those two years, and cannot drink any alcohol on or off duty for the rest of their lives. Every guard spends five hours a day getting his uniform ready for guard duty. For the first six months of duty the guards cannot talk to anyone, and their off-duty time—all of it—is spent studying the 175 notable people laid to rest in Arlington National Cemetery. These are people such as Presidents Taft and Kennedy, and Medal of Honor recipient and movie star Audie Murphy, who was also the most decorated soldier of World War II. Those guys have way more discipline than I would ever have.

After viewing the changing of the guard, Mike and I joined back up, and walked through more of the cemetery grounds. One thing that struck me was the notations on the headstones.

One in particular really made me stop in awe:

"William Quinton, Brigadier General of the US Army, 1836-1916." And below his name was, "His Wife, Martha Newburgh, 1842-1915."

Then, just behind that gravesite, was this headstone:

"William Warren Quinton, Major, United States Army, 1870-1943," then, "His Wife, Cornelia Bentley Sage, May 16, 1936," and "Beloved Daughter, Pauline Elizabeth Quinton, April 9, 1990."

I don't know why this hit me the way it did, but to see an entire family with memorial plots together was just inspiring. Another one I saw that struck me as very respectful was a site for Thomas Selby Collins, who was Vice Admiral of the United States Navy in World Wars I and II. His headstone listed his accomplishments, but below his name and credits, was this inscription:

Wife—A Gallant Lady
Agnes Williamson Combs

It was the only headstone I saw with that particular inscription—A Gallant Lady

Very cool.

One thing about Arlington: It is quiet. There is a sign posted near the entrance that says, "Welcome to Arlington National Cemetery, Our Nation's Most Sacred Shrine. Please conduct yourselves with dignity and respect at all times. Remember these are hallowed grounds."

On the day we were there, it was busy. There were a lot of people doing the same things we were—walking around, looking at the headstones, classes on field trips, a couple of funerals, and such. But, it was quiet.

Respect is huge to a biker, and this place was oozing respect. I am convinced that one cannot go to Arlington without getting emotional. I do not know anyone buried in Arlington and, as the one reading this, you may not either. It does not matter. We have the freedoms and life we have in the United States because of these people.

And they have my eternal respect.

July 22

Because of the weather, we hit the road early again, rolling out of Annapolis on US 50 about 6:30 a.m. The heat wave was continuing, with no signs of letting up, and the news had mentioned that 34 states were under severe weather advisories at that time. We were in the middle of it.

We went across the Annapolis Bay Bridge, and down to Ocean City, Maryland, which is the end of US 50. We had noticed, looking at the map, that US 50 just skirted Delaware by about two miles, and we decided we could visit Delaware, even if it was only for ten or twelve miles. We turned off US 50 onto Route 54, and rode the ten miles to the town of Delmar, whose motto is, "The town too big for one state." This town sits literally on the state line between Maryland and Delaware, and we were there long enough to get a picture or two in front of the sign, and buy a lottery ticket. We could honestly say that we went to Delaware on our trip, even if it was only for five minutes.

Then we saddled up to go five miles back to US 50. We hit Ocean City about 30 miles down the road, crossed the bridge, and parked at the Boardwalk. By now it was about 9:30 a.m., and topping 95 degrees, again with the 90-plus-percent humidity. Of course, we had to walk a block or two back to the bridge and get a picture of that highway sign: "Sacramento CA 3073," just like the one back in California.

Mileage sign

Outside of Ocean City, Maryland

The next couple of hours were spent wandering a bit through the tourist trap shops and looking at the boardwalk. I walked out to the beach. I was in blue jeans, boots, my cut and a tank top—a little overdressed for the beach. Then I put my hand in the Atlantic Ocean.

Yeah, I know, I should have gone in. But skinny dipping on Ocean Beach was likely frowned upon by the local law enforcement community. And, if I had gone in wearing my jeans, I would have steamed myself dry on the ride out of there, being that it was so hot.

I talked for a couple of minutes with a lifeguard on the beach. He told me that the heat and humidity was so intense there that week, that people would come to the beach in the morning. But, by a little after noon or 1:00 p.m., it would start to empty out, as it was too hot even for the locals. I walked back to our bikes, and we got back on the road. We had to run west on US 50 back a few miles to Highway 113, then we caught Highway 13 south for the remainder of the 110-mile trip to the Chesapeake Bay Bridge and Tunnels.

A quick side note: The trip across the Chesapeake Bay Bridge and Tunnels was not really considered in our initial planning of our trip. But, one night I was watching Discovery Channel, and they were talking about the history and construction of this massive project. About halfway through the show, I called Mike and said, "We need to ride this bridge." And, of course, he said, "I was planning on it." And, so we did.

The bridge, officially the Lucius J. Kellam Jr. Bridge-Tunnel, is commonly referred to as "CBBT." It is a toll bridge, which costs $12 to cross, that spans—oddly enough—Chesapeake Bay. More than twenty miles long and four lanes wide, the bridge crosses the bay, and then drops into two one-mile-long tunnels beneath the Chesapeake Bay and Thimble Shoal navigation channels.

The bridge was originally completed in 1964, with a second, parallel structure built in 1999. Because of the distance across the bay, engineers could not build a regular bridge high enough to allow shipping traffic through, and to withstand the weather conditions. Building a drawbridge was hardly even considered, as the draw spans would have been too large and numerous. Also, it was not prudent to close the shipping lanes—mainly because the United States Navy, in addition to all the commercial shipping traffic, crossed the bay regularly.

Hence, the bridge-tunnel combination was developed. The project was called one of the seven engineering wonders of the modern world in a worldwide competition following its opening in 1964.

One of the amazing things that occurred to both Mike and I as we rode across this massive span, was that, in the middle of it, land was no longer visible.

We paid our toll, and rode onto the bridge in fairly moderate traffic. It's weird. The initial approach to the bridge, and the first span of it, was just like any other bridge—a short span across Fisherman's Inlet; then we crossed the Fisherman Island National Wildlife Refuge. No access from the roadway to the island exists.

The island was about a half-mile from the eastern shore of the Virginia National Wildlife Refuge and was the southernmost barrier island. The island was originally estimated at just less than 1,900 acres in size, but sand kept expanding the island's acreage. The refuge is home to numerous birds such as herons, egrets, osprey, and shorebirds, as well as being a resting and feeding spot along many other species' migration routes. A coast survey in 1852 appeared to be the first accurate map of the island, which, at the time, was about 25 acres. All of Virginia's other barrier islands are shrinking in size, but Fisherman's Island continues to grow.

After we crossed the island, we rolled back out over the water, and rode about six miles before we began to drop down into the first tunnel. A mile later, we came back up to the bridge deck.

Looking around, all we could see was ocean. No land. The span over the water continued for about another fourteen miles, and we eased down into the next tunnel. This is when it occurred to me: We were essentially riding under the ocean. It was a weird feeling, not claustrophobic by any means, but just intriguing.

I have ridden tunnels under water before. The one that immediately comes to mind is the George Massey Tunnel under the Fraser River just south of Vancouver, B.C, which always had amazed me. But this was so much more amazing.

As we came out of the second tunnel a mile later, we saw a turnoff for the visitor's center and rest area next to the Sea Gull Fishing Pier. Since we were in no hurry, we pulled off to grab a drink and cruise the gift shop.

The fishing pier is located on the southernmost of the four man-made islands along the CBBT, and extends 625 feet into the bay. Sitting just over three miles from the mainland at Virginia Beach, the pier has a certified weighing station and cleaning station. And no fishing license is required. Shark, blue fin, flounder, trout, and much more, are caught from this pier, which is free to everyone after paying the initial bridge toll. For non-fishermen, the rest stop also has a restaurant, photo vantage points and viewing machines, an interpretive display showing the construction of the CBBT, a gift shop, and a set of exhibits showing Naval history provided by the Hampton Roads Naval Museum.

We hung out for about an hour or so, and then decided to head on up to our friend's house in Gloucester. We eased back onto the road and, as we came off the southern end of the bridge, and away from the water, the heat went up dramatically, and we could feel it climbing.

We had been stopping about every hour as it was just to go into a convenience store, or whatever, just to cool off. And, as we merged onto I-64 into Norfolk, Mike heard on the radio that it was 103 degrees. In the Pacific Northwest, we have wind chill, which is used in the winter. It could be 30 degrees out, but with the cold wind, your body feels much colder. Here, they had a heat index, which means your body feels more heat due to the humidity. With the heat index, because of the humidity in Norfolk, it felt like 125. They were right. It was miserable. Rolling along in the left lane on the interstate, we were cruising along nicely, sweating like crazy, and looking forward to seeing our friends in Gloucester. .

That's when we hit the traffic jam. And traffic was stopped dead.

We were surrounded by idling vehicles, in 103-degree weather. Waves of blistering heat rolled up from the asphalt and from our air-cooled engines. We inched forward a few feet, and then stopped again. This went on for about ten minutes until we saw an electronic reader board above the freeway that said, "Accident ahead 7 miles." Mike and I looked at each other, said something like, "screw this," and began working our way to the right shoulder.

A little aggressiveness, and some very polite drivers, allowed us to creep over onto the shoulder. No, we weren't stopping to let the bikes cool down. We were going to ride the shoulder. But, you say, that's illegal. Yep, sure was. It wasn't the first time I had done something illegal. And, it would not be the last, either. I didn't care. A $100 (*or whatever*) ticket is much better than heat stroke and a $5,000 motor.

So, we cruised up the shoulder for about six and a half miles until we saw the accident. We eased back into traffic, and idled past the scene. Then we opened up the throttles, and made our way to a gas station, where we bought cold bottles of water. We drank some, poured some over our heads, and hung out in the air-conditioned store till our poor scoots cooled down. OK, we really didn't hang out in the store, as much as we hung out in the walk-in beer cooler. We sat on cases of Budweiser, drank our water, and got a very strange look from the beer delivery guy who showed up. Oh, yeah, we cooled off, too.

Armed with some cold water in our drink bottles, and tanks full of gas, we headed out of Norfolk up to Gloucester, where we successfully found Eric and Julie's house about 5:00 p.m. Thank God their house had AC, and the fridge had cold beer. We got our gear off the bikes, got set up in the guest room, and took long showers to get the sweat, road grime and gunk off our bodies.

July 23-24

Up to this point, since leaving home, we had covered 4,500-plus miles. We had originally figured on taking about two weeks to cross the country so, even though our schedule pretty much went out the window on the second or third day, we were still doing well. We had planned on touring Jamestown and Yorktown while we were there—might as well see some culture. I've never been one to spend days on end in museums and attractions. When I'm on the road, just being on the road is the attraction for me. I love the countryside, the views, the small towns, and so on, as I ride. Granted, some places are just things one should not pass up (*i.e.-Arlington National*

Cemetery), so we did spend some time doing the whole tourist bit, cameras and all.

Eric and Julie were our tour guides, and our first stop was Yorktown. The Yorktown Battlefield and Visitor's Center is a national park with tours of General Washington's headquarters and Surrender Field. It is also the site of the Yorktown Victory Monument and Moore House, where the surrender terms were negotiated. A recreated military encampment and a simulated 1780s farm site were also set up on the property.

Mike and his new friends

Yorktown, Virginia

Virginia's colonial government established Yorktown in 1691 for the purpose of regulating trade and collecting taxes on imports and exports for Great Britain. The population grew to almost 2,000 people by the early 1700s, and was a major port and economic center. Storehouses, docks, wharves and businesses dotted the waterfront, while homes and other businesses were scattered throughout the town on the bluff above. When British General Lord Cornwallis arrived in Yorktown in 1781 to establish a naval base, General George Washington's forces besieged the British Army. On October 19, Cornwallis surrendered. By the end of the war, much of Yorktown had been destroyed, and the census of 1790 noted only 661 people remaining.

There was a farmer's market of sorts set up along the waterfront, and we wandered through that for a bit, then walked down to look at some schooners and ships docked at the wharf. Colonial homes still stand on the bluff above, including the home of Thomas Nelson, Jr., commander of the Virginia Militia during the siege, and a signer of the Declaration of Independence.

After seeing what there was to see, we drove out to the Grand French Battery. This battery and redoubt occupied a section of about 1,000 feet from east to west, and contained 30 pieces of artillery, which assaulted the British forces over a half-mile away. In August 1781, British Lieutenant-General Cornwallis started to fortify the area, and on September 28 the 17,000 men of the allied army of French and American forces marched to Yorktown to siege Cornwallis' stronghold of 8,000 men.

The allied army (*French and American Forces*) built its first siege line on the night of October 6, 1781, which ran from the Grand Battery to the York River. The battle began on October 9 when the allied forces opened fire on British forces.

On the 11th, allied troops attempted to make a second siege line, but were stopped by two British earthen forts blocking the way to the York River. The night of October 14 saw quick victory for the allied troops, when the French attacked Redoubt 9, and Americans attacked Redoubt 10, seizing both positions in less than a half hour.

On October 18, officers from both sides met at the home of Colonel Augustine Moore for the negotiation of surrender of the British Army. Amazingly, some of the cannons and mortars still stand, intact and complete with their manufacture dates of 1756 and 1777 clearly visible.

By this time, we'd had enough of the heat and being soaked with sweat, so we all piled back into the car for the ride back to the house. Along the way, we managed to stop at the Harley dealer for souvenirs, and then hit a local restaurant for cold beer and good food. Back at Eric and Julie's place, many beers were consumed, and many lies and tales of the road were told. Problems of the world were solved, and we finally called it a night.

We walked out of the house the next morning and, as soon as we stepped outside, we were immediately drenched in sweat, and our cameras and glasses got fogged up. Great. Another muggy day. Our destination was Jamestown and Jamestown Settlement.

Your next history lesson: In 1607, thirteen years before the Pilgrims landed at Plymouth, more than 100 English men established Jamestown, the first permanent settlement in the colonies. It was the capital of Virginia until 1699. The colony was sponsored by the Virginia Company of London, which was a group of investors hoping to make a profit from the venture west (*times haven't changed much, have they?*). Problems soon began to arise in the settlement, which was in the middle of about 14,000 Algonquin Indians led by Powhatan.

Even though relations were weak, trading was established between the two parties. Disease and death became common in the settlement, because of a poor water supply, unfamiliar climate, lack of food and a prolonged drought. Since many of the original settlers were from upper-class England, the colony had few skilled farmers and laborers. Settlers attempted a number of small industries to make money, but it wasn't until 1613 that tobacco was introduced as a cash crop, and it stimulated the growth of the small colony.

It was also in Jamestown that the first documented Africans in Virginia began to arrive in 1619 from Angola in West Africa. It was not long before these indentured servants became slaves and, in the second half of the seventeenth century, these slaves became the primary source of labor.

Many parts of the original settlement are still standing, or are in the process of restoration. Most notable is the brick church built in 1608. The church was also the site of the wedding of Pocahontas and John Rolfe in 1614. In addition, we saw an excavation site of the burial plots and the old barracks. Memorials dating from the 1600s to the early 1900s dotted the area.

A visitor's center (*air conditioned!*) had many more exhibits and artifacts to see. After roaming through that, it was time to head home before we all died of heat stroke.

Aaahhhh…more cold beer and air conditioning.

CHAPTER SIX

HEADED SOUTH
July 25-26

And away we go.

Back on the road again, we headed for Richmond, then down to Afton, which took us to the start of the Blue Ridge Parkway. We took off from Eric and Julie's early, after drying off our bikes—which were soaked from the insane humidity—and topping off the tanks. We had to make a quick stop in Richmond at a Fastenal store to make an attempt at fixing my cup holder, which was falling apart.

Of course, the damn thing required a special screw, and I figured Fastenal would be the ones to have it. I was right. We found the place, went in, and showed the guys behind the counter what we needed. They fixed me right up. At no charge. I got the cup holder fixed while Mike and the Fastenal guys chatted about our trip, then off we went.

Thankfully, as we headed inland toward Richmond, the heat and humidity subsided, and it was at least tolerable. Getting back on the highway was an adventure, as people in Richmond don't know how to drive, (*sorry, Richmondites*). After stopping at the Harley shop, and refueling our scoots, we made our way to the Blue Ridge Parkway. The map had shown us that there was a small town about 35 miles down the road called Buena Vista, (*usually pronounced, "bway-na vis-ta"—this is important*). So we set our sights on that for the night.

Start of the Blue Ridge Parkway

The town sits in a valley a couple of miles off the parkway, and we wound our way down to look for a motel. We passed one on our way into the downtown area, and cruised through beautiful downtown Buena Vista before returning to the aptly named Buena Vista Motel, and getting a room.

Typical hijinks ensued—unpacking the bikes, turning the AC to frostbite, having a shot of whiskey, and washing the road grime off our faces.

A side note: Almost all of the motels we stayed in used white linens and towels. After cruising for 200-plus miles in sweltering heat, through construction zones, traffic and bugs, it is amazing what happens when you wet a white washcloth and wipe your face.

Yeah, they're not white anymore. And some of the ones we used will never be white again.

But, I digress. We rode back into town to find some dinner, and decided the old Pizza Hut converted to a Mexican place sounded good, if nothing more than for a frosty Margarita.

It was a little after 4:00 p.m. and, as we rolled up to the place, we noticed it was closed. The sign on the door said they opened at 5. Really? OK, well, it was a small town after all. As we fired up the bikes again, however, the manager poked his head out the door and told us to come on in if we wanted.

Damn fine idea.

We sat down and ordered a couple of Margaritas, browsed the menu, and then ordered. The Margs went down way too easily, so we politely asked them to bring two more. They were happy to oblige and, by the time we got our food, the place was filling up with other diners. I think it was here that someone mentioned our bikes outside, and the Washington license plates…something to the effect of, "You're a long way from home."

So we told them a bit about our trip, and complimented them on their town (*it really was a nice little place*), and when they asked if we were staying in town, we told them the Buena Vista Motel. That's when the lady said, "Oh, no, it's "By-oona Vis-ta."

Ummm, OK. Never heard "buena" pronounced that way before. But, hey, it's your town.

Anyway, we finished our grub and decided against that third Margarita, since it's always been bad form to wobble and fall over on a bike, especially so when you're 4,500 miles from home in a small town.

Upon returning to the motel, we noticed a group of riders on Yamahas was just unpacking their gear into the rooms next to ours, so we chatted a bit. It turned out they were from Cincinnati, and we ended up sitting outside the rooms for a good portion of the night talking about what we love—riding.

Yeah, here comes another side note: One of the things I truly love about being on the road, besides the ride itself, is when I can meet other riders on their own road trips. This has happened more often than not, and is one of many reasons why I like to stay in the old motor-court-style motels. I have had some great nights in small towns like Buena Vista—Wenatchee, Washington; Nelson, B.C.; and more—just talking to other riders and even non-riders who just love to hear of the adventures of being on the road.

We were up and on the road about 7:30 the next morning and, while it was foggy in beautiful Buena Vista, the temperature was still in the mid-70s. We climbed the three or so miles back to the Blue Ridge and, at the stop sign at the parkway, three huge deer jumped out of our way not ten feet away from us.

We began our trek on the parkway, and I can tell you right now: There are simply no words adequate to convey how gorgeous this ride is. The fog cleared as soon as we rose out of the valley, and we saw wildlife and scenic views that took our breath away. Of course, we stopped at the turnouts to take pictures and go, "Ooh-aah, isn't that pretty," then rolled on. Someone had told us to be sure to stop at Otter Lake, about 25 miles down the road.

As we rolled up to it, there was no second-guessing. We had to stop. The lake was clear, and smooth as glass. Everything was still and quiet, as it was still fairly early. Being as it was a Tuesday morning, there was almost no traffic. The lake spills over a small dam into a stream that eventually feeds into the James River. With cameras in hand we walked down along the stream, not wanting to say anything lest we break the morning stillness.

Otter Lake

Along the Blue Ridge Parkway, Virginia

Soon, we realized we had been there for almost an hour, and not one other vehicle had gone by. So we mounted up, kicked the bikes into gear and rolled on, stopping here and there for views of the valleys below. We could literally see for miles and, at this point, we were only about 3,000 feet up.

After a few more stops, we suddenly realized we had been on the road for almost three hours, but had travelled only 50 miles. Oops. OK, new game plan. Let's not stop at every overlook we come to. The really nice thing was, we left the stifling heat and choking humidity behind us, and the weather was perfect.

So, back on the parkway, we wound our way through the sweeping turns, tight curves, and tunnels. We dodged the occasional pheasant, and passed under beautiful, arched bridges. We enjoyed views of the river below, and the mill ponds with their still-operating waterwheels. We made a couple of stops at these for pics, and then we came to the Mabry Mill.

Located officially in Meadows of Dan, Virginia (*such cool names out here*), the Mill was built by Edwin Mabry between 1903 and 1910 as a water-powered grist mill, blacksmith shop and sawmill. It ceased operation in 1935. Today, National Park Service volunteers give craft-making demonstrations. Self-guided tours include soap-making, kettles, and an old whiskey still. Paths were abundant on the grounds, and views of the mill itself, the log flume, and the surrounding area were amazing. There was also a restaurant and gift shop on the site as well.

Mabry Mill

Along the Blue Ridge Parkway

Our next stop was at the Rocky Knob Information Center, run by the Park Service. The lady behind the counter, Barb, was awesome—very helpful and knowledgeable. Mike and I had wanted some patches or pins or something from the Blue Ridge Parkway, but Barb said they were out, and she was waiting for more to come in. She told us, however, to put our names and addresses down, and she would make sure they mailed us a couple of patches when they got them in.

We did spend some time at the visitor's center, not that it was this huge building that took an hour to walk through it. The building itself is quite small. But we wanted to get some of the history of the parkway, and how it came about.

The idea for a scenic route along the Blue Ridge Mountains spine first came about in 1906. President Franklin Roosevelt, during a visit to Shenandoah National Park in 1933, was impressed by Skyline Drive, which was under construction at the time. Senator Harry Byrd, from Virginia, suggested building a mountain road that went all the way to Great Smoky Mountains National Park. Roosevelt was interested, and Byrd obtained backing from officials in Virginia and North Carolina.

As part of Roosevelt's New Deal to create jobs during the Great Depression, $4 million was initially allocated in November of 1933 to commence building this mountain road. On September 11, 1935, a team of about 100 workers started clearing and grading land on Pack Murphy's farm, which became the first section from the Virginia-North Carolina border to Cumberland Knob, about twelve miles south.

Very little of the land was unspoiled, having been farmed, timbered or commercialized, which meant that literally thousands of trees had to be moved, along with tons of dirt and rocks. The first work contract paid men 30 cents per hour. They worked six days a week, and most of the early labor was all done by hand.

This was also the first of 45 segments of the parkway, which runs from Rockfish Gap, Virginia, on the north. It then connects to Skyline Drive and Shenandoah National Park, and runs a total of 470 miles to Cherokee,

North Carolina, which is also the eastern entrance to Great Smoky Mountains National Park.

The road twists and turns over mountain crests, through farmlands, and drops into river valleys on its way south. The Blue Ridge crosses four major rivers, six mountain ranges, and more than 100 gaps, which are areas between mountains. Elevations on the parkway run from 649 feet in southwest Virginia to 6,047 feet in North Carolina near Mount Pisgah. That variety in elevations and landscape means there is a large range of ecosystems along the road as well.

The first 50-mile section of the road was opened in April of 1939, and roughly two-thirds of the road was completed in 1942. Construction was halted, however, due to World War II. Construction resumed after the war and, by 1967, all but the Linn Cove Viaduct section in North Carolina was completed. There are no billboards, stop signs, or traffic lights along the entire length of the parkway, and utilities are buried. Mile markers appear regularly, and signs are very few and far between. There are regular entrances to the Blue Ridge, but they are unobtrusive and offer no hint of civilization. A posted speed limit of 45 miles an hour is in effect for the length of the road. But most of the time we were doing less than that, just to take in the scenery.

The park service has restored and added attractions over the years, including the Blue Ridge Music Center (*midway through the park*), which is an outdoor amphitheater for concerts; the Johnson Farm, a 1930s-era history attraction; and the Mabry Mill. In addition, numerous small towns along the way have capitalized on their musical and arts heritage to become artistic destinations themselves, such as Asheville, North Carolina, and Floyd, Virginia.

After leaving the mill, and the Rocky Knob Information Center, we rode down to Fancy Gap. Yes, it's a town. There are a lot of Gaps around here. And, with our mental state of twelve years old, we had a lot of fun with some of those names (*Lick Log Gap...hee hee*)!

We had actually booked a room in a motel, supposedly in Fancy Gap. As this was the tourist season, and we were in a tourist trap area, motel rooms could be hard to come by. We could not find the damn place. We asked a few questions, a few times, at a few places, and finally found the Volunteer Inn and Lodge on a dirt road, in the middle of nothing, eight or so miles out of town. Add to that, there really was not much in Fancy Gap as it was. There were no restaurants. Those were in the next town over, called Hillsville.

We made a command decision to bail on the place, and rode into Hillsville, about six miles north of the Blue Ridge. We secured a motel room at the Knob Hill Motor Lodge, a really nice-looking motor-court-style place run by this little 80-something-year-old lady and her dog.

They had a room, thank you very much, for $55. This room was probably one of the nicest, if not the nicest, we had stayed at during the entire trip. It was old, but amazingly clean, and large, and had the most comfortable beds ever. We had noticed a Coke machine next to the office, and decided we should have a drink to celebrate, well...whatever we wanted to. So we went to fill the ice bucket, and buy a couple of Cokes. They were 50 cents each. Wow, we can't hardly buy a six-pack of Coke in the stores for 50 cents each. In addition, being in the Bible belt, we noticed that there was not only a Bible on the nightstand, but it was open to the Book of Job. Praise the Lord, and pass the butter!

So after our usual unpacking, washing, and looking at a map of the town, we decided to head in for dinner. We had seen a place called Aunt Bea's, so we thought we'd try that out. Part of the reason is that Hillsville is just down the road a piece from Mount Airy, North Carolina, which we knew from the old "Andy Griffith Show" when we were kids. Mount Airy was always the big town that folks in fictional Mayberry went to. So, anything that purported to be related to Aunt Bea we just had to try.

Unfortunately, the cafe looked to be a glorified fast-food joint, and we wanted something more like real food. We motored on down the road, and found a shopping center that also housed a Mexican place, a sports bar, and a steak house. Steak it is.

We had a decent meal. It was not overpriced, and the service was good. Our bellies full, we scampered back to the motel, poured a drink, and sat outside until it got dark. The motel sat on a hill in town that overlooked a valley (*mostly businesses and warehouses, but still a view*), and it was a gorgeous night for sitting outside.

Mike said it best, "It does not matter how many pictures you take, how many words you use, how big of a vocabulary you have, there is simply no way to adequately describe the Blue Ridge Parkway."

It is phenomenal.

July 27-28

No words. As I said earlier, there are no words that can describe the beauty of the Blue Ridge Parkway. We had an easy day rolling along this amazing road, taking tons of pictures, getting hit by tons of bugs, and generally stopping whenever we felt like it.

We crossed from Virginia into North Carolina and, of course, made a stop at the state line. It's an actual state line. Yes, there is a sign that says, "North Carolina State Line." But there is also a white line painted across the roadway at exactly that spot. Yes, we got pictures of us straddling it. The weather was perfect—mid-80s, a few fluffy clouds floating lazily through the sky—and there was very little traffic. We rolled through, and stopped to enjoy the views at, places like Cumberland Knob, Stone Mountain State Park and Green Knob, which was at 4,760 feet elevation.

Virginia–North Carolina State Line

The one thing we noticed about this day's ride was that the scenery, once we got into North Carolina, had changed. It was still beautiful, but not as scenic as the prior day's ride. Wildlife was much more abundant, or at least much more visible, and we had to dynamite the brakes more than once as deer and smaller animals suddenly appeared next to or in front of us.

There was a place we came across called Linville Falls, which had a visitor's center, and snack bar. So we dropped in there to maybe grab a sandwich, and take a bathroom break. Yeah, snack bar my butt. All they had was a little gift shop setup with candy bars, chips and junk food.

We did take advantage of the bathrooms, saddled up, and thought we would just hit a little town called Spruce Pine, about twenty miles away, and maybe five miles off the Blue Ridge. Of course we missed the turnoff, and rather than backtrack, we opted to keep rolling toward Asheville.

All along the Blue Ridge there are small cemeteries dotting the landscape, some right next to the road, and no bigger than a quarter-acre. Curiosity got the better of me, and on one of our "ooh-ahh, isn't that pretty" stops, I told Mike that the next one we saw I'd like to stop at it. Sure enough, not five miles later, we saw one on our right, adjacent to the Blue Ridge Baptist Church. We eased off the road into the church yard, parked our scoots and grabbed the cameras. This wasn't a large cemetery by any means, but was very well-tended, and sat right in front of the church, between it and the road. The driveway up to the church building curved slightly, and it bordered the graveyard with its white split rail fence.

As you may have guessed from our visit to Arlington, headstones interest me and, while nothing overly memorable was on these, the dates are what piqued my interest. Obviously, church members and their families are buried here, with births dating back to 1847. The majority of the headstones seemed to be for family plots. Some sites were simply marked with only an in-ground headstone, while others were quite ornate with large marble monuments. It was a very interesting place.

Mike had seen in the dealer directory that there was a Harley store about six miles east of the parkway in a little town called Swannanoa along US 70, so we stopped in for souvenirs, and to cool off a bit. The afternoon heat was building toward the mid-90s by this time and, since we had not stopped for lunch, it was a good time to locate some grub. Across from the Harley store was a pizza joint, so we hopped over, had a great lunch, and refilled our water bottles.

Mike and I always carry water bottles with us, especially on long trips, as it's easy to get dehydrated when you're riding. And, if you get really dehydrated, as I did one time in the Canadian Rockies, it's no picnic. My body ached like I had the flu, I had a headache that would not quit, and just generally felt like crap. Ever since that trip, I always carry a water bottle. The nice thing is that every mini-mart, fast-food joint, or restaurant we have ever stopped at to ask if we could refill our water has said yes.

From Swannanoa, we made our way into Asheville to find a motel. We really did not want to traverse the entire city looking for a place, and our information said there was a Super 8 only about six miles from us. After about a half hour of looking, we gave up, and found a hole-in-the-wall called the Thunderbird Motel.

It was not the worst place we had stayed, but it was close. If you looked up "dive motel" in the dictionary, it would have a picture of this place. It was old, and not updated in any way, but it did have AC and a television, and was next to a convenience store-gas station. The other attraction was that it sat back off the road a bit, and we parked the bikes right in front of our room.

Morning arrived for us about 6:00 a.m., and we were packed up and on the road by 7:00. We had to make a stop to air up the tires, top off the gas tanks and hit our standby, Mickey Ds, for a quick breakfast. Three miles later we were sailing down the Blue Ridge once again, headed toward Maggie Valley.

The Blue Ridge through this part of North Carolina was higher than we had been, and we were stopping at overlooks such as Beartrail Ridge, 5,072 feet, and Licklog Gap, 5,135 feet. As we rounded a curve near Milepost 395, we came upon a small tree that was down across the southbound lane. Since there was no traffic, we easily got around it, and pulled off at the next overlook a few miles further down the road. The National Park Service had a phone number to call to report various incidents, and we dug out the map, located the number and called.

Of course, the first number we tried would not work, as all I got was a rapid busy signal, as if the line was out of order. There was a second number listed as well, so I tried that one, and got a recording that basically gave generalized information about the area. Alrighty then. We hit the road and, about ten or so miles later at our next photo stop, I tried the numbers again with the same results. OK, sooner or later they would find out about the tree. I had tried to do my civic duty.

A few miles later, after climbing and climbing, we came across Milepost 431, and saw the sign indicating the highest point on the Blue Ridge parkway at 6,047 feet. The turnoff sits at the Haywood and Jackson county line, and offers an amazing view of the valleys below.

Naturally, we stopped for pictures and to chat with some of the other riders who were there, taking pictures in front of the sign. One group of riders was from Ontario, Canada. A woman in their group mentioned that we should watch out for the pack of dogs that was roaming the road just down from the summit.

A pack of dogs? That's something we hadn't seen yet. Sure enough, as we were there, these three dogs came walking up the road toward us. I could tell they were not wild dogs, as they had radio collars on, but they also were not cared for—very skinny, and they were hungry. Thankfully, they were also friendly, and came right up to us. We got some water for them and, between the various riders at the viewpoint, we were able to dig up some crackers and snacks for them to eat. I looked, and saw that the dogs had nametags with the owner's name and phone number and, surprisingly enough, I had cell service.

I dialed the number, and this good ol' boy answered. He was really surprised that I had his dogs. Ol' Bubba Joe Jim-Bob said he had someone out looking for them. He asked where we were, and said he would get up there to grab them. Other riders had rolled in by this time, and we let them know what the deal was with these poor dogs. Since the dogs seemed in no hurry to leave, we decided it was time for us to move along.

Roughly 75 miles after leaving Asheville, we turned onto Highway 19 and rode the five miles or so into the town of Maggie Valley, which is the home of the Wheels Through Time Transportation Museum.

This place is cool. Established in 1993 by Dale Walksler, the museum is home to tens of thousands of motorcycle photos, memorabilia and artifacts. It is considered to be the premiere collection of rare American vintage motorcycles, with more than 300 vehicles in the collection.

Everything from Harley-Davidson, Indian, Excelsior, Crocker, Henderson, and more, was on display, along with a few vintage automobiles, and even an airplane or two.

Mike and I

The "Wheels Through Time" Museum

The museum was fairly busy, and we spent hours walking through the exhibits and displays, until we stopped and started talking to a couple of guys at one exhibit next to us. They asked about our trip, mentioning they had always wanted to do a ride like the one we were on. Our advice to them was, don't wait. Do it as soon as you can.

We happened to be talking to them next to an old sidehack that definitely had seen better days. A lot of the bikes at WTT are not restored, or are partially restored, and this one had not yet seen any signs of a restoration. One of the museum employees came up. He had overheard our conversation, and he said, "You know, most everything in here runs." He then took a few steps over to the bike, kicked it once, and fired it off. He didn't let it run for more than a minute or so, as the building, large as it was, would have filled with exhaust and fumes. But it did run, and fairly smoothly.

It turned out he was Dale, the owner of the museum, and he told us a little more about the exhibits and memorabilia he had. After we had finished wandering through the building, we headed outside to find some lunch, and Dale was out front talking to a few people. We went up to thank him, and he asked where we were from. Mike told him we were from Washington, and gave him a brief rundown of our trip.

"Well, hold on," he said, "I'll get Hailey to take a picture of you for our Facebook page." Sure enough, this little cutie comes out a minute later with camera in hand. So we posed in front of our scoots and had our pictures taken. Dale wished us luck with the rest of our trip, and recommended a local sports bar for lunch. So off we went.

After lunch, we hopped back up to the Blue Ridge Parkway for the final leg of it. The Blue Ridge ended about fifteen miles out of Maggie Valley at Milepost 469, where it crossed the Oconaluftee River, and intersected with US Highway 441.

Last milepost

Blue Ridge Parkway, North Carolina

We rode through Bryson City, and made our way into the town of Robbinsville. We had made reservations at the Two-Wheel Inn about three miles outside of town, and located it without much trouble at all.

This was a really cool place. It's not much on design, as it looked almost like a bunch of self-storage buildings as you rolled up to it. The rooms were good sized, very comfortable, with AC and satellite television. The coolest thing was they had a garage attached to each room for our scoots.

We checked in, got the bikes unpacked, and opened the door to our room. Uh-oh. One bed. That isn't gonna work. Mike trotted up to the office again, and told the lady behind the desk that we needed two beds. We were close friends, but not that close. She said she would be right down. And, folks, sure enough she wandered down, went into our room and pulled the bed apart. It turned out the bed was two twin beds shoved together. Quick as a flash, she had the two beds made back up with new sheets and blankets, and was on her way.

Well, that's when we realized we were out of refreshing adult beverages. It was time to hit the liquor store. Being that Robbinsville is a small town, about 600 people, we asked the owner of the motel where the liquor store was in town.

"There isn't one," she said.

Huh? No liquor store?

"This is a dry county, and you're in the middle of it."

Great. It turned out that not only was it a dry county, it was the only dry county in the whole damn state. The nearest liquor store, she said, was about twenty miles away in Topton, just over the county line. As much as it pained us to say it, we were not going to ride another 40-plus miles for a bottle of whiskey.

Live and learn. Next time we roll through a town and we are low on booze, we're stoppin'. Anyway, we visited with some other riders from New York who were staying at the motel. We all went into town for dinner. Then we sat outside in the evening heat, and had a great time talking about riding and travelling.

July 29

The Tail of the Dragon

We lit out from the motel a little after 7:00 a.m., hit our usual McDonald's in Robbinsville for a quick breakfast, then rode the rest of the twenty miles or so to Deals Gap and the start of the Tail of the Dragon.

Deals Gap is home to the Dragon, a section of US Highway 129 at the North Carolina-Tennessee border. It is now considered by many people to be the world's best motorcycle and sports car road. It boasts 318 curves in the eleven-mile stretch, and has only two intersections in fourteen miles—NC28 that goes to Fontana Dam, and a little-traveled gravel road at Parsons Branch.

The surrounding area is fairly remote, and most of the road is bordered by the Great Smoky Mountains

National Park, US Forest Service property, and land owned by Alcoa Aluminum. The 318 curves that are the road's claim to fame are on the Tennessee side. Deals Gap is actually the gap in the mountains that the road follows and, at the state line between North Carolina and Tennessee, it is the highest point on the Dragon, at just less than 2,000 feet.

The Dragon's past is rich and notorious. It was originally an animal track used by the Cherokee Indians, trappers and hunters in the early 1700s. A crude roadway, Parsons Branch Road, was built in the early 1800s in order to access the settlement of Cades Cove. It remains a gravel road to this day. Landowners began collecting tolls for the use of the road, and about halfway over the Dragon is Toll Booth Corner. It is said that some who tried to cross without paying the toll were hanged on the spot.

In the late 1920s the Dragon took on some new designations—TN72 on the Tennessee side, and NC288 on the North Carolina end. A bridge built near Tapoco in 1931 joined highways NC288 and NC108. The two highways were paved, and were renumbered as US Highway 129 in 1934. Even then, the highway was lightly used mostly only by locals and lost tourists for the next few decades.

Coming in from North Carolina, the Dragon starts at Fugitive Bridge, where you can see the Cheoah Dam. The dam is mostly famous for the scene in the 1993 movie "The Fugitive," where Harrison Ford jumped into the river below. From there, the Dragon climbs through a steep series of "S" curves called The Slide, then levels out and straightens until another collection of turns near the Crossroads of Time, a motel-restaurant. Then Deals Gap and the Tennessee state line come into view. And for the next eleven miles it's nothing but curves, turns and twists.

Three other movies besides "The Fugitive" have been filmed along the Dragon. The first was "Thunder Road," a 1958 film about moonshiners starring Robert Mitchum. One of my favorite movies, "Two Lane Blacktop," from 1971, was also filmed here, and features scenes of the state line, the old Esso gas station, the original one-lane bridge at Tapoco Dam, and more. A 1988 film called "In Dreams," starring Robert Downey Jr. and Annette Benning, had scenes at Calderwood and Cheoah dams along with a chase scene between the Dragon and Fontana.

We got to Deals Gap just about 8:00 a.m., as the store was opening for the day. Being as it was a Friday, we had hoped traffic would be light, as we had heard that the Dragon can get pretty jammed up on weekends. We were right, although there was this huge Winnebago-style motor home just heading north through the Dragon as we got there.

The store had just opened, so we went in and looked around for a few minutes, mainly to give Mr. Rolling Condo a chance to get ahead of us. The last thing we wanted was to be stuck behind some mega-camper around the twisties. After about ten minutes, we figured we should get rolling, as a group of Mazda Miatas were assembling in the parking lot for their chance at carving up the corners.

We headed off, grabbed a photo of the sign at the state line, and then began motoring our way through the turns. We were in no hurry, and took our time easing through the twisties to get a feel for the road, and the layout of the turns. Our plan was to ride the Dragon three times— once northbound, then southbound, and finally northbound again, to continue on into Knoxville.

The turnout at milepost nine proved a great spot to stop, take a couple of pics, and talk about the run so far. At the end of the Dragon, the road straightened out, and ran alongside the lake. The next turnoff was about a mile or so after the road evened out, along Calderwood Lake, and we pulled off there to head back the other way.

This was where the fun began. We had figured out the lay of the curves, the condition of the road and so on, so we could run it a little faster this time. We switched places, and Mike led as we headed south toward Deals Gap once again. We still never got past third gear, and mostly were in second the entire run. We leaned into the turns and twists enough that our floorboards, and Mike's exhaust, were scraping on almost every lean.

Whenever we ride, whoever is leading always constantly checks the mirrors to make sure the other is still back there, hasn't crashed, or broken down, or whatever. Mike mentioned, when we stopped again, that he never once had to check his mirrors for me; he could hear my footboards scraping on most every turn!

Carving a turn

On the Tail of the Dragon

One interesting thing we noticed was that on a couple of the corners there were guys with cameras taking pictures as we wound through the turns. Back in Deals Gap, the pictures are available for sale. It took a couple of days for our pictures to hit the respective photographers' websites but, when they did, they were awesome. I think I ended up buying six or seven of them. We picked up a couple of posters and souvenirs with the intention of mailing them home, but the gift shop does not do that. We had to run the twenty or so miles back to the Robbinsville Post Office. So we did.

Then someone told us about the 36-mile-long Cherohala Skyway, which crosses the Cherokee and Nantahala National Forests into Tellico Plains, Tennessee. Completed in 1996 after 34 years of construction, it is the most expensive highway in North Carolina—costing $100 million. It climbs up and over the 5,400-foot mountains before descending another 21 miles into the backcountry of Tennessee.

From Robbinsville, we rode to Santeetlah Gap, and climbed to the overlook at 5,390 feet, then cruised along the mountaintop the remaining seven miles to the state line. Visibility was decent most of the time but, unfortunately, we were in the clouds, with even a little rain some of the time, so the spectacular views we had been told about were not possible. Once we hit the state line we dropped into the Tellico River basin, then into the town of Tellico Plains.

It was a pretty, neat-looking town and, as we dropped into the town along the river, the temperature had climbed into the high 80s. We saw a Harley shop along the left side of the road, so, naturally, we stopped in. We discovered it was basically a T-shirt shop for the tourists, way overpriced of course, and owned by one of the Harley dealerships in Maryville, Tennessee, about 40 miles away.

We visited with the girl behind the counter for a bit, and asked her if there was a decent place to eat in town.

She said to try the Nuthin' Fancy restaurant just up the road, so we thanked her and scooted off. She was right, it was about a mile away, and we pulled up to a red and white classic-styled building, with a huge front porch. The place was called Nut-n-Fancy. Even better, they had a sign out front that said, "Biker Friendly."

They had home cooking, killer food, and probably the best peach cobbler I had ever eaten. The service was exceptional, and the prices were very reasonable for the amount of food we got.

Even better, we had the entire place to ourselves. Once we had stuffed ourselves, we topped off the tanks at the Chevron next door, and were back on the road toward Knoxville. With the thermometer climbing into the mid-90s, and the humidity returning with a vengeance, we rolled into Knoxville, and found a motel.

We had planned on staying two days here, not because Knoxville is one of those places we really wanted to hang out in, but because the bikes needed servicing. I had called the Harley shop to schedule our services, and found they didn't take appointments, but only dealt on a first-come, first-served basis. So, after checking in, and unpacking the scoots, we headed off to find the shop and see what time they opened in the morning.

Located in a converted auto dealership, Knoxville Harley-Davidson had a separate shop area from the main store. As we wandered through the showroom, Mike trotted back to the service department and found they could do our services right then and there, and have us done by the end of the day. "Great," we said (*or something like that*), and rolled our well-traveled babies back to the shop.

The store had a waiting area with television and a pool table, so we hung out and played pool for a couple of hours. I even let Mike beat me a few games.

Back to the motel we went. On the way, we stopped at the liquor store for a much-needed replacement bottle. We then informed the motel clerk we would be staying only the one night.

The clerks at the shop had told us that Coyote Joe's was a good place to grab dinner. A lot of the guys from the shop hung out there, and they have good food. They had even told us that the place gets packed on the weekends, that we'd have trouble finding a seat, since it was Friday night and all. There were a lot of bikers, cold beer, blah, blah, blah.

We got there about 8:30, walked into the, so far, not-crowded bar, and sat down. The cute bartender without a bra on, Leeann, came over and took our drink orders and, when we asked for a menu, we were told the kitchen wasn't cooking anything. It was too hot in the back. We could order sandwiches, salads, stuff like that. We didn't really know what to order, so we asked her what she would eat. She told us she would have the guys make something up for us, and off she went.

A few minutes later, she trotted out with a couple of toasted sandwiches that were absolutely grubbin'. We wolfed those down along with a couple of beers, listened to the rednecks at the bar, and way too much country music. Then they started setting up for karaoke, which was our clue to leave.

We headed back to the motel, and saw what looked like a party at another bar. This one was outside on a patio adjacent to the bar-restaurant, and they even had a live band. We whipped in and parked, walked up to the doorman, and were promptly told we couldn't come in because we didn't have sleeves on our shirts.

WTF? Hillbilly boy can barely wear shoes, and he wouldn't let us in without sleeves? Hell, I don't think he even had teeth. Who knew that Tennessee would have a dress code?

Thank God we had whiskey in the motel.

CHAPTER SEVEN

NORTHBOUND

July 30

We got out of Knoxville (*Thank God!*) on I-75, and rolled across the state line into London, Kentucky. There was a Harley dealer along the road we were on, the Hal Rogers Parkway. We had never heard of Hal Rogers, but he had to have been a big shot to get the former Daniel Boone Parkway renamed for him.

Sure enough, Hal Rogers had been a United States Representative for Kentucky's 5th District beginning in 1981. The Daniel Boone Parkway was originally built as a toll road in 1971 and, through Rogers' effort in securing $13 million in federal funds, the toll was discontinued and the toll booths removed in June of 2003. The highway was renamed in honor of Mr. Rogers by former Governor Paul Patton as thanks for removing the tolls. Local residents, as well as descendants of Daniel Boone, were outraged that the roadway was renamed for, according to the Associated

Press, "someone whose primary accomplishment" was getting tolls lifted from a 63-mile-long highway.

We stopped in at Wildcat Harley-Davidson just before they opened and, once inside, discovered probably the friendliest bunch of employees we had seen on the entire trip. We chatted with some local riders as well, and told them we were planning on running north on Highway 30. They told us where to turn to catch the road, but said, "Make sure you ride the new 30, not the old one."

OK. Highway 30 turned out to be a nice, smooth, mostly two-lane road through Kentucky farmland, with some nice scenery...at least, for about twenty miles. We came to an intersection and, following the instructions we had been given, we made a right turn. We were still on Highway 30, but we almost instantly found ourselves on a narrow one-and-a-half lane road with twists and tight turns, very rural, and a lot of dead cars and trailer houses.

We made our way into a small town called Booneville, and stopped to refill our water bottles and check the map. Ideally we wanted to go to Beattyville, which appeared to be less than ten miles away. I think almost every little town and off-the-main-road burg in Kentucky had to be named something-ville, because it seemed they all were.

We saddled up, kicked the bikes into gear, and were off. We rolled along on Highway 30, cruised leisurely along, and then came to the realization that we had gone about 20 miles. Yet we thought that Beattyville was less than ten. *Hmmmm.* Then we saw the sign for Beattyville. OK, then. We're good. It turned out we were supposed to catch Highway 11 somewhere along the way (*that we both missed*), and now we were headed the long way to town on Highway 52.

Even still, it was a nice ride through places like Lone, Tallega, and St. Helens. Yes, places, because there were no towns there, just highway signs announcing that was where we were.

We got into Beattyville, gassed up, and looked at the map again (*not that it had helped before...*) enough to realize we had stayed on Highway 30 way too long. Because of that, we had made a 48-mile detour instead of the direct nine-mile route we had wanted. Oh well. It was a good thing we had no schedule.

We mapped out our escape from Beattyville (*essentially back the way we had come*) and decided it was time for lunch. We found a place called Kaydee's Kitchen in downtown Beattyville. Town was essentially a bunch of mostly empty old buildings, an auto shop and some antique stores. But Kaydee's was a great little café with sandwiches, salads, and such, on the menu. It was owned by Alisha Lucas, and the restaurant was named for her daughter. It was decorated with tons of old movie posters, album covers, and musical instruments.

We sat down, and noticed the basket of peanuts on the table, so of course we started munching on those. When Alisha, the owner, came over, she said, "Oh, you can just throw the shells on the floor." It felt kinda funny doing that, since the whole place, including the floor, was so clean you could probably eat off it. But, being the good guests we were, we tossed shells on the floor until our lunch came.

We headed out of town on Highway 11, and made a turn onto the Bert Combs Mountain Parkway, named for the former governor who was instrumental in building the 75-mile section of US 460 through the mountains. The road was in great condition, and we made good time rolling along at about 70 miles an hour. We were headed toward I-64 and into West Virginia for the night.

We sailed through, or past, towns like Salyersville, Paintsville, Ulysses and Louisa before jumping onto the Interstate. Just before crossing into West Virginia, we came across a major industrial area that housed power plants, a nuclear plant, oil refineries, and so on. It was an interesting sight, as they just appeared as we crested the hill.

Someone had been kind enough to turn the thermostat up, and it was getting hot and muggy again. We pulled over to get a picture of the "Welcome to this state," sign and put our brain buckets back on, as West Virginia has a helmet law.

Mike's back was killing him, and we decided to get off the road as soon as we could. We hopped off the freeway a few miles farther down, and found a Super 8 motel. It was a bit of an adventure getting checked in, as the computers were down, and they couldn't really do much of anything without them. Finally, the clerk tossed a couple of rooms keys our way, told us what room we were in, and said they'd figure it out when the computers came back online.

It was time for a drink—and Tylenol for Mike.

July 31

Fog. A lot of fog. Could-barely-see-across-the-parking-lot fog. We packed up the scoots, availed ourselves of the free breakfast at the hotel, and rolled down the hill to gas up.

After filling the tanks, Mike hit the starter on his Road Glide and...click. Nothing happened. One more time, and click. This brought a few colorful words out of his mouth, and I told him I thought it might be a loose connection at the battery. We pulled the seat, got the tools out and, sure enough, I was able to get about a quarter turn on the positive cable. Mike hit the button, and the bike roared to life. He reassembled his bike, and I got the tools stashed, and off we went.

It kind of pissed us off that our bikes had just been in for service in Knoxville, and the cable had not even been checked, which is standard procedure for any service on a Harley.

Anyway, we cruised through Huntington and onto Highway 7 into Ohio. The fog finally began to lift as we rode along the Ohio River and, being as it was Sunday morning, we had almost no other traffic, and the countryside was just gorgeous. It was mostly a two-lane country road that skirts the river on one side, and farmland and houses on the other, with a lot of old barns and outbuildings in various states of decomposition.

One little town that stood out was Gallipolis, a very cool, old town. It had an old movie theater on Main Street—the whole Americana thing going on. Just past the main downtown area (*as much downtown as a village of less than 5000 people can have...*) we came into the new area—a shopping center, strip malls, fast-food joints, and such, that ruin a small town.

We cruised out of town along the river, and the farmland suddenly gave way to this huge power plant and nuclear plant run by American Electric Power. Based in Columbus, Ohio, AEP owns the nation's largest electricity transmission system, covering nearly 39,000 miles, and serving 5,300,000 customers. Of course, we grabbed a few pictures, then continued through Cheshire and Coolville (*no shit...that really is the name of the town!*) onto I-77, and headed north toward Cleveland.

We popped into Adventure Harley-Davidson in Dover for a potty break, and to grab an extra quart of oil (*always good to be prepared*), then it was back onto the superslab for the run into Cleveland.

As we were zipping merrily along I-77 about a half hour or so, we saw a road sign for the next exit, and the Pro Football Hall of Fame. We briefly pondered making the stop, but there were a few reasons we didn't. One, it was already getting toward late afternoon, and we still had to find a motel in Cleveland, about another hour away. And two, neither of us are big football fans (*gasp! What sacrilege!*),so spending two-plus hours and $22 to walk around and look at exhibits we really weren't interested in seemed kind of senseless to us. And, it turned out the whole place was freshly under construction for a huge expansion project.

The Hall of Fame was started in 1963 with seventeen charter members, and now boasts more than 260 members. Unlike other halls of fame, officials are not eligible for induction. The location of the hall is significant, as the National Football League was founded (*as the American Professional Football Association*) in Canton in 1920; and the city of Canton lobbied successfully to have the NFL build the museum there.

Construction began in the summer of 1962, and consisted of one building of 19,000 square feet. A $620,000 expansion project broke ground in the spring of 1970 to increase the size of the hall to 34,000 square feet, which included a pro shop.

Yearly attendance at the Hall also passed the 200,000 mark about this time. The next expansion was started in the fall of 1977, at a cost of $1.2 million. The year-long project included an enlargement of the gift shop, theater, and research library, and expanded the Hall of Fame more than two and a half times its original size to over 50,000 square feet.

In July of 1993, the Hall of Fame announced yet another expansion, projected to cost over $9 million. Completed in late 1995, this project included the "Game Day Stadium," a 20 by 42-foot Cinemascope screen, which shows NFL films. At the time we rolled past, it was expanding from 85,000 square feet to over 118,000; as well as renovating 37,000 square feet of the original building.

Included in the renovation are a new main entrance and lobby, a special exhibition gallery for temporary exhibits, a renovation of the 50-year-old rotunda, an expanded retail store, and indoor and outdoor spaces for special events, private event rentals, and so on.

Inductees to the hall are selected by the 46-person board of selectors, comprised mostly of sportswriters. To be eligible for nomination, a player or coach must have been retired for at least five years. Induction is limited to seven persons per year. An exhibition game, called the Pro Football Hall of Fame Game (*wonder how they came up with that name?*) is held annually the day after the induction ceremony, and officially starts the NFL preseason.

But, as I said earlier, we kept rolling past to see if we could find a decent place to park for the night. We ended up about an hour north of Canton in an outskirt of Cleveland called Beachwood, near Shaker Heights. We found another Super 8 Motel that was older, but very well-kept, and reasonably priced. The temperature was pushing the low 90s by the time we hit the motel. Our plan was to stay a couple of days in Cleveland, as we wanted to hit the Rock and Roll Hall of Fame.

The desk clerk told us where some of the restaurants were in the area, and we opted for the Cheesecake Factory for dinner. It was a little more spendy than we cared to pay, but it was well-worth it. This place put out good food, and a lot of it, and made a decent drink to boot. It was located in an upscale shopping center that had yuppie stores galore, and fancy bistro restaurants. But it's hard to beat the Cheesecake Factory.

Next, the Rock and Roll Hall of Fame.

August 1-2

Wow. It started out as kind of a lazy morning, we were in no hurry to rollout and hit the road, as we were mainly staying in the area. The museum opened at 10:00 a.m., so we took our time getting up, having breakfast, and so on. We made sure the camera batteries were fully charged up, and took off on the twenty-mile, or so, ride into Cleveland. This was a cool town to ride into. As we neared the city, the buildings just seemed to grow, and the summer sun gleaming off the facades of the skyscrapers was really something to see. Then the lake appeared. Lake Erie just seemed to go on forever, and the water was a deep blue sparkle as we rolled into town.

Cleveland is a bustling city of almost 400,000 people, and ranks as the fifteenth largest combined metropolitan area in the United States. It was founded in

1796, and is perched on the south shore of Lake Erie at the mouth of the Cuyahoga River. For this reason, it quickly became a hub of manufacturing and shipping.

Over the years, Cleveland earned a reputation as an industrial town with steel mills, automotive plants, and rail and shipyards. The 1960s and 1970s saw a decline in Cleveland's population, as suburbs and outlying areas grew. However, the mid-1980s ushered in a revitalization that still continues.

As it developed a diverse economy, Cleveland earned the name, the Comeback City, and has set a standard for urban planning. Five major industries have grown to be the economic strength of this region: Biotechnology, science and engineering, medicine, education, and manufacturing. The Cleveland Clinic Health System is considered a world-renowned treatment center, and has served dignitaries from around the world.

It is also home to the second largest performing arts center in the United States, and has the nation's first health museum, the Great Lakes Science Center, a world-class orchestra and, of course, the Rock and Roll Hall of Fame. It also has numerous honorary consulates from around the world. In 2005, Cleveland earned the designation as one of the most livable cities in the United States.

Mike and I made our way through downtown, one of the cleanest and nicest I have ever seen, and found ourselves on Rock and Roll Boulevard staring at the Hall of

Fame. It took a few minutes to find a place to park, and we walked the few blocks back to the museum.

If you are a music fan, this place is a must see. Just like a biker needs to experience Sturgis at least once, a music lover has got to experience this museum.

The museum began to take shape after the formation of the Rock and Roll Hall of Fame Foundation in New York City more than 25 years ago. A poll conducted by USA Today ranked Cleveland as the best location, and the location was made official in May of 1986. The eye-catching building was designed by renowned architect I.M. Pei, who freely admitted he knew nothing about rock and roll. The ground-breaking ceremony was held on June 7, 1993, with attendees such as Billy Joel; Atlantic Records president, Ahmet Ertegun; "Rolling Stone" magazine publisher, Jann Wenner; Chuck Berry; Pete Townshend of The Who, and more.

It was at this ceremony that Townshend donated his Gibson J-200 guitar to the museum, the same one he used to compose the legendary rock opera "Tommy." In 1994, Yoko Ono donated a huge collection of artifacts from John Lennon to the museum, including the guitar used at the 1965 Shea Stadium concert, the leather jacket he wore in Hamburg, and lyrics handwritten by Lennon.

The museum officially opened on September 2, 1995, with a ceremony that ended with a benefit concert at Cleveland Municipal Stadium. The performers included Chuck Berry, Al Green, Aretha Franklin, Jerry Lee Lewis,

Johnny Cash, John Mellencamp, the Pretenders, the Kinks, Lou Reed, and many more. More than eight million visitors have been welcomed by the museum since its opening.

Be prepared—it's not cheap. And, it's not a quick tour. But it is well worth the $22 admission. We got there just as the museum opened, and made our way into the six-story structure. Photos are allowed only in the lobby and the atrium area immediately downstairs. The main entry is on the second floor and, from the lobby-atrium area, we went downstairs to the first floor of exhibits.

The first thing I saw was a Porsche painted in psychedelic colors that had belonged to Janis Joplin, and a Harley-Davidson Sportster owned by Billy Joel.

There were also small exhibits of artifacts and instruments from blues greats Sonny Boy Williamson, Howlin' Wolf, bluegrass legend Bill Monroe, Johnny Cash, and even Lady GaGa. It's almost overwhelming to see everything they have housed there.

We went through the doors from the atrium into the exhibit area, and it was almost sensory overload. The exhibits were well-placed, but also had multimedia and listening stations that told the history of the particular artist or era as we looked at them.

A huge Elvis Presley display had a small movie screen hanging above one of his famous Cadillacs showing a loop of his concerts. There were also his stage costumes, guitars, records, awards, and much more. We wandered through the multitude of exhibits: Queen, The Who, Creedence Clearwater Revival, Dr. John, the Beatles, Jimi Hendrix, and more. We weren't rushing through them, and we didn't get to see everything. Two and a half hours later, we thought we had better see some of the other five floors of stuff.

We hiked up to the little cafeteria upstairs for a bite to eat. They had overpriced $6 sandwiches, and processed, microwave food. Then we went into the theater area just outside the café. This small theater shows non-stop film clips of the inductees by year. We sat through about four years' worth—not that it took four years. We were there for about a half hour.

We walked out of the theater, then went up a darkened, curved hallway with a backlit wall. On this wall were the etched signatures of every inductee in the hall of fame. Upstairs, we came to the exhibit at the time, "Women in Rock." There were displays and artifacts from Bessie Smith, Mahalia Jackson, and Aretha Franklin, all the way up to Queen Latifah and more. We went around another corner, and saw the original Sun recording studio that Elvis had recorded in, and the studio that Alan Freed broadcast from.

Once we were back outside the museum, we saw a bus in the front of the building with a small sign sitting next to it. We strolled over, and read that it was Johnny Cash's tour bus, the JC Unit One. Cash had this bus built to his specifications, at a cost of $553,000, and used it for the last twenty years of his career, from 1980 until 2003. He sold the bus three months before his death and, after a series of owners, the bus was bought by Dave Wright on eBay in 2005, who then donated it to the museum.

Johnny, June and their son John all had personal compartments on the coach, with television and stereo in each one. And, personalized it was: The table in Cash's bedroom is built from salvaged wood from Ulysses S. Grant's headquarters. In fact, some of the wood used in customizing the bus came from Cash's plantation in the Bahamas.

At the time, it was illegal to harvest and export the wood off the island, so Cash had crates built from the wood, shipped items back to his home in those crates, and then took the crates to the coach builder for use in the bus itself. You gotta love a rebel.

The bus was even used for the Highwaymen tour in 1991, with Cash, Willie Nelson, Waylon Jennings, and Kris Kristofferson.

By the time we made it back out of the museum, and had finished with Cash's bus, (*yes, people are allowed inside!*), we had thought about going next door to the Great Lakes Science Center. However, it was getting late in the afternoon, and we were pretty-well wiped out from all the exhibits, (*sensory overload?*) and the skies were darkening.

In addition, we really did not want to get tied up in a lot of rush-hour traffic in the 90-degree heat on air-cooled bikes. With the clouds building, we figured we may be in for a late-afternoon thunderstorm. We were wearing what we were wearing—no coats, no helmets, just our boots, blue jeans and T-shirts.

We made our way out of town (*Cleveland has got to be one of the easiest towns to navigate*) and onto the Interstate for the run back to our hotel. It was a fairly slow ride out of downtown, as the commuters were already on the road, but nothing like we encountered back east. Forty-five minutes or so later, under darkened skies, we pulled into the parking lot, and got into our room.

About fifteen minutes later, we heard the first thunder boom, and saw the flash of lightning. Then the skies opened up. This was not rain. This was a deluge of biblical proportions. Big fat drops of rain came down so hard they were literally bouncing inches off the pavement. They created a whirlpool torrent of water that circled the storm drain in the middle of the parking lot. Thunder continually shook the building, and lightning lit the sky like fireworks on the Fourth of July. The storm passed after about an hour or so, and the sky was bright blue, with not a cloud to be seen.

Thunderstorm

Cleveland, Ohio

We decided to walk across the street to Bahama Breeze for dinner. It was kind of a yuppie place for my tastes, and we weren't sure how they would react to a couple of road-grizzled bikers (*not that we cared either*), but the place was really cool. We sat in the bar, and the bartender was great. He made good recommendations on the food. They had great drinks, and reasonable prices. And, the food was fantastic. A lot of times these chain restaurants have mediocre food, ridiculous prices and poor service. Not so here.

Back in the room, Mike and I did battle with the bottle of Crown, and talked about our day. We're not sure who really won the battle. There was whiskey left (*not much*), and so I'm considering it a tie.

The next morning we headed out under beautiful blue skies, hit I-90 eastbound, and stopped about 60 miles later for gas and breakfast. We skipped through Pennsylvania, and into New York.

There is a funny thing about New York. They need a sign that says, "Welcome to New York. Now Pay Up." Toll roads are everywhere. We paid the toll for our passage, and made our way into Buffalo on our way to Niagara Falls. Our plan was to go to the Canadian side of the falls, as we had heard the view is much better from that side.

Our stomachs were grumbling a little, and we decided to just grab a quick bite. So Mickey D's it was. I know, we should have had Buffalo Wings at a bar somewhere, right? But, as I said, we just wanted a quick bite to take the edge off. Thank God for the dollar menu. So, a small, tasteless hamburger and Coke later, we were back on the road, gassed up and headed over the Peace Bridge into Fort Erie, Ontario.

Mike and I

Entering Canada

We got through customs with no trouble at all, and rode the Niagara Parkway along the Niagara River from Fort Erie all the way into Niagara Falls. The town of Niagara Falls is straight up a tourist trap, and parking is a bitch. There are two public parking garages in town, one at each end of the town, and they screw you for $20 for a place to park.

No way in hell were we going to fork over that kind of money to park for an hour or so, so we cruised the town looking for alternatives. Normally, on my scoot, I will make my own parking spot and call it good. Being in a tourist trap town, in Canada, with Royal Canadian Mounted Police crawling all over the place, the last thing we wanted was our rides impounded for illegal parking.

We found a casino-restaurant-tower viewpoint kind of thing at the top of a hill with parking available, and the sign said "$10." We eased up to the gate, and asked the attendant about using one spot for both bikes. "Oh, no," he said. "They're too big. They won't fit." When we countered with something like, "B.S., just watch us," he relented, took our $10 and let us in.

There was a path leading from the parking lot down through a small wooded area onto the main street through town. Across the street was the walkway and viewpoints for the falls. It was not far, maybe a few hundred yards or so, and we trotted across the street to the walkway.

Being as it was a beautiful, hot summer day, the place was crawling with tourists and sightseers. Our cameras worked overtime getting shots of the falls, the people, and the views. The sheer amount of water cascading over the falls and into the river below was breathtaking. We looked down into the river, and could see the little sightseeing boats dwarfed by the falling torrent of water.

Niagara Falls is actually three waterfalls straddling the United States-Canada border: Horseshoe Falls, American Falls, and Bridal Veil Falls. Horseshoe Falls is the largest of the three, sitting on the Canadian side of the border, dropping about 175 feet. The tourist information states that it is also the most powerful waterfall in North America.

American Falls, on the American side (*obviously...duh*) has a drop of about 100 feet, and is separated from the Canadian side by Goat Island.

Mike and I

Niagara Falls

Bridal Veil Falls is also on the American side and is the smallest of the three waterfalls. The three falls tumble into the Niagara River, which drains Lake Erie into Lake Ontario. It is estimated that because of the volume of water roaring over the cliffs, the land underneath erodes at the rate of about one foot per year.

We stood at the various viewpoints along the walkway, and we could feel the spray from the water as it

136

fell into the river. And we were quite a distance from the falls themselves.

Our original plan had been to grab a motel in St. Catherine's, Ontario, about fifteen miles from Niagara Falls. After seeing the prices, and how much of a tourist trap that area was, we opted instead to ride farther inland, away from the river and Lake Ontario. Besides, it was hot and muggy, and we wanted to cool off with a nice highway breeze. We hiked back up to the parking lot, and went into the casino-restaurant-gift shop-tourist attraction that was at one end of the lot, grabbed a Coke, and hung out in the AC for a bit.

We rolled out of town on Queen Elizabeth Way for about 40 miles, enjoying the ride along the southern shore of Lake Ontario. As we rode away from the lake, we turned onto Red Hill Valley Parkway, and then the Lincoln Alexander Parkway (*What's the old joke? We drive on a parkway and park on a driveway?*).

I will tell you, the Province of Ontario really needs to do a better job of labeling their highways. We would see a sign at an intersection or an exit—not before the intersection, mind you—telling us that we needed to turn. But, of course we were not in the turn lane.

When we did make an exit, there were no signs telling us where we should go to get onto the road we wanted. I swear we made more damn U-turns between Niagara Falls and Brantford than we did on the whole trip before this.

Fortunately, when we found ourselves in a neighborhood and stopped to get out the map, a resident came out and gave us directions back to the highway. OK, it included an illegal turn or two. But what the hell. They're only illegal if you get caught. Right? After we hit the highway again, we rolled on for about another fifteen miles until we came to the town of Brantford.

We had to stop to fill up anyway, and decided to see if this would be a good place to stay. There was a tourist center across from the gas station and, after we topped off the tanks, we headed across to see if we could get a city map and find a motel. We wanted something besides the Best Western, Hampton Inn, or Days Inn chain hotels along the freeway.

The attendant inside was very helpful, and told us those hotels were way over $100 a night for a room. Then she told us exactly where we should go to find some local motels and restaurants.

She also gave us some history on the town. Populated by almost 94,000 people in the city limits, and over 135,000 in the metropolitan area, Brantford was home to Alexander Graham Bell, and was where he invented the telephone.

The first distance phone call was made from Brantford to Paris, Ontario, in 1876. More recently, Brantford is known as the home of hockey great Wayne Gretzky, and the late comedian Phil Hartman.

Leaving the tourist center, we motored south across the highway, and turned onto Colborne Street in a small business district bordering the neighborhoods. About a half-mile down we saw the Sherwood Motel, an older motor court motel built in the 1950s, but very nicely kept. They had a room for $75 a night. We took it. We backed our scoots into the spots in front of our room, unloaded, wiped the sweat and grime off our faces, and had a drink.

Dinner was starting to sound like a damn fine idea, and there was a restaurant right next door to the motel that looked like it was built about the same time. We walked over, and had a great home-cookin'-type meal before making our way back to the motel. The Weather Channel was our favorite television show that night, as they had been calling for thunderstorms and rain the next day across southern Ontario and Michigan—right where we were headed.

CHAPTER EIGHT

LAKESIDE RIDING

August 3

Tim Hortons. As I've mentioned before, McDonald's was our usual choice for breakfast on the road, mainly because of the dollar menu. In Canada, however, there was no dollar menu. Besides, Canada had Timmy's. Tim Hortons up north were about as prevalent as Starbucks in Seattle. They were everywhere.

Anyway, we packed up the bikes and checked out of the motel. We then gassed up, popped into Timmy's for a donut, and hit the road. It had been raining overnight, and the streets were still a little wet, but the skies looked pretty good. We had been watching the Weather Channel on television at the motel, and they had been calling for showers throughout Southern Ontario. But, when we headed out, it was dry. That is, until about fifteen miles out of Brantford.

It started with a few sprinkles, then some bigger drops, and then it became real rain. Now, it wasn't so much the rain that was bothering us, it was the road spray from the semis and other vehicles on the freeway. And traffic was fairly heavy, making the spray that much worse. Mike and I pulled to the side of the road under a bridge, and grabbed the raingear, suited up, then motored on down the highway once again. Of course, anyone who rides will immediately know what happened next. The rain stopped. Well, really it was about ten miles down the road, but still…

We kept our gear on just because of the road spray issue, and because it looked like we may be hitting some more rain before we got out of Ontario. We soon came to the Bluewater Toll Bridge, which took us over the St. Clair River and into Port Huron, Michigan. This bridge is nothing spectacular from a design standpoint, but it is almost 6,200 feet long. It is the second busiest crossing point between the United States and Canada. The Ambassador Bridge between Windsor, Ontario, and Detroit is the busiest. Naturally, this meant we had to go through customs at the United States end of the bridge.

The border crossing in the westerly direction had eight lanes leading up to the guard shacks where they checked our passports. We motored into position in one of the lanes, and waited. And waited. And waited. Then we waited some more. Fortunately, we were on a downhill grade, so we shut the bikes off and rolled forward every time a car made it through customs.

And Murphy's Law was in full effect as we waited. The line we chose was the slowest moving one of the eight lanes, mainly because Border Guard Joe had to inspect and search damn near every vehicle that crossed his path. We did have time to strip off the raingear and stow it in our packs. And we had a nice chat about our trip with a dude in a BMW next to us.

At one point, about 30 minutes into our wait, we noticed an Ultra Classic roll up behind us and head over toward Lane 7—we were in Lane 4. You guessed it; he made it through the border crossing easily fifteen minutes before we did. By now, Mike and I were thinking we're going to be in for the inquisition of a lifetime. Our bikes are going to get searched, our packs are going to be scrutinized. Hell, a cavity search was not out of the question the way this guard was searching.

Finally, we made our way to the crossing, and Mike went up first, since he was leading the ride that day. A few seconds later, the guard motioned for me to come up as well, so I eased up next to Mike. The guard looked at the passports, asked how long we had been in Canada, and told us to have a good trip.

Like I said, Murphy's Law: 80 minutes of waiting, and a minute and a half to get through. I suppose Border Guard Joe figured we couldn't hide a dead body or 50 pounds of drugs in our saddlebags.

The clouds had parted somewhat by this time, so we pulled into a quickie mart/gas station to refill our water bottles, and top off the gas tanks once again.

We headed north out of Port Huron on Highway 25, following the shoreline of Lake Huron. This was a great road, and a nice easy ride. But it didn't always offer a view of the lake, as the road eases away from the shore in places to allow for the McMansions along the waterfront. Highway 25 follows the thumb along the lake. It goes north, then curves at Port Austin, and heads southwest-ish along Saginaw Bay toward a town called Bay City.

My Shadow

Somewhere in Michigan

Our plan was to ride to Port Austin, about 200 miles or so from Brantford, but the ride was so easy and the weather was dry and mild, so we kept rolling. We did stop in Port Austin, and had lunch at a sports-bar-type place. Coming out, there was just enough of a breeze coming off the lake that we put our jackets on. The views along the lakeshore were spectacular, with views of the lake, farmland, and small-village-type towns, and so on. The temperature had climbed again once we headed into Bay City, at the south end of Saginaw Bay, about 65 miles from Port Austin.

Rolling through Bay City, we looked for a motel, and stumbled across a Harley dealer that we hadn't expected to see. Great Lakes Harley-Davidson was a small store sitting on the edge of the highway at the end of town with very friendly people. We bought our souvenirs and headed back out to the bikes.

I noticed a barber shop next door. My hair was getting a bit shaggy, so we stopped in, and I got my hair buzzed off by a little cutie. When we trotted back out to the bikes, Mike's wouldn't start...again. It was the same thing as in West Virginia, it would just click. He popped the seat off, I got the tools out, and this time we discovered the negative cable was slightly loose. I cinched it back down, he put the seat back on, and we were good to go. (*Thanks again, Knoxville Harley...*)

We ended up at the Euclid Motel back in town, a brick motor-court-style that we liked so much, with restaurants and stores all within walking distance. Dinner was at the Chinese buffet restaurant in the strip mall next to the motel and, after stuffing ourselves silly, we walked back to our room to grab a drink and sit outside.

As we walked back to the room about 6:30, however, we noticed some clouds building in the distance over the bay. Not a big deal, but these had some strange, and beautiful, colors to them. The weather report was showing clear and warm for the next day, so we didn't think much of it. Sitting outside, that all changed.

These clouds, as they headed toward town, got darker, meaner and angrier as they moved forward. The colors got brighter and more vivid, with grays, oranges and greens all tumbling over one another. After about ten minutes we could see the wall of rain that was plummeting out of the sky, and the wind was picking up. Mike went back into the room, and pulled up the Weather Channel on his computer. He looked at the satellite picture for the area, and saw...nothing. Clear skies. He hit refresh on the screen and updated the image. The satellite picture from ten minutes prior was clear as a bell, no storms, no rain, not even clouds. About five minutes later, as the storm was preparing to roll over the top of us, I was measuring the doorway and the handlebars to see how we were going to put the bikes in the room.

The other patrons of the motel had long disappeared into their rooms, but Mike and I (*not the sharpest knives in the drawer*) were in front of our room taking pictures. As the mass of clouds rolled over on top of us, it turned the early evening as dark as midnight. Then the wind ceased, the storm moved along, and it sprinkled a minute bit of rain. It was not even enough to be called rain, more like a mist. Twenty minutes later the sun was out, the temperature was back up, and it was like nothing had ever happened. It was the weirdest thing we had seen during the entire trip.

August 4

We got on the road under sunny skies after a bite at Mickey D's, and a quick stop at Tim Hortons (*gotta love a town with both Mickey's and Timmy's!*). We headed out of Bay City on Highway 13, then onto Highway 23, and rode north along the shoreline of Lake Huron once again. We cruised easily through small towns and farmland and, at one point, we noticed a sign for a lighthouse, but were rolling too fast to stop for it. A little further up the road, we saw another sign, giving us a little more warning for the 40-Mile Point Lighthouse. We pulled off the road, and made our way down the short road to the lighthouse compound. Sitting on 22 acres, the lighthouse was still in operation. The light shines for fifteen miles.

The history of the lighthouse and surrounding compound was interesting. Beginning in 1889, plans for a new lighthouse started to take shape. Congress authorized the project in 1893, but never appropriated the $25,000 needed to fund construction. Finally, the plans were approved, and contracts were awarded to build the lighthouse and signal. The property was purchased, and work began in 1896. The first structure erected was a wood-framed building for housing the work crew during construction. Still standing, the building is now the gift shop.

The lighthouse itself is 52 feet high with a twenty-inch-thick foundation. Construction was completed on November 12, 1896. It was too late in the year to activate the light, so the board hired a temporary caretaker to stay at the light in one of the apartments that was built at the base of the tower. The first keeper arrived in January of 1897, and the lighthouse was manned by official lighthouse keepers until 1944, when the United States Coast Guard took over the maintenance and operation of the station. On August 16, 1971, the reservation became a county park known as Lighthouse Park. Presque Isle County assumed the responsibility of maintaining and preserving the lighthouse and building. The Coast Guard is still in charge of maintaining the light. The site became part of the National Register of Historic Places in July of 1984.

We toured the lighthouse and the keeper's cottage, which has been restored to its original state, with furniture, kitchen appliances and supplies from the late 1800s and early 1900s. The tour guide in the lighthouse told us they were preparing to re-wire the electrical system, as the light had a tendency to flicker at times. After touring the lighthouse and the cottage, we made the short walk to the beach.

This part of Lake Huron is known as the "Graveyard of Ships," because, as of 2006, more than 1,200 wrecks have been recorded. The lake has more than 3,800 miles of shoreline, and contains 30,000 islands, including the world's largest freshwater island, Manitoulin Island. A major storm in 1905 was responsible for 27 wooden ships being lost. A portion of the hull from the steamer ship, Joseph S. Fay, can still be seen about 200 feet north of the lighthouse. Surprisingly, for the size of Lake Huron, the water was fairly warm. Not that we went swimming; we just touched the water to see how warm it was.

We got back up to the bikes, saddled up, hit the road, and made our way around Hammond Bay along Highway 23. Lunch was starting to sound like a damn fine idea and, after about 35 miles, we rolled into a little town called Cheboygan. We spotted an Irish pub on Main Street, and thought we might try that. We pulled up, backed our scoots to the curb, and hopped off. I turned around, and saw we were parked in front of a little café called the Step Inn. Still wary of local Irish pubs after our West Virginny fiasco, and knowing that northern Michigan may not be any better, we decided to step in to the Step Inn.

Honestly, it was one of the best choices we had made on the whole trip. It was totally a mom and pop type of operation. The hostess greeted us right away, got us seated, and poured us each a glass of water before our butts hit the seats. I know it was lunchtime, like 11:30ish, but breakfast sounded good to me, and I ordered an omelet. There were a few other customers in the place, and we chatted with the hostess and the busboy while we waited for our order.

I think they should have used a forklift to bring it out. The omelet was very fresh, cooked perfectly, and huge. So big, in fact, that it hung off each end of the plate. The menu said it was a three-egg omelet, I think they must have been ostrich eggs. Then there were the potatoes and toast. Not some frozen shredded hash browns, these were cut potatoes that were seasoned to perfection. It was by far the best omelet I had ever eaten, and it was less than $10. Even the chef came out and talked with us for a bit.

After our immense breakfast-lunch, we hit Highway 23 again for the short run to Mackinaw City, which is the end of Highway 23. We stopped in the small village to look around, and grab some photos. They even had a Harley store there, but it was mainly a T-shirt and souvenir store. Home to only 850, or so, people, the village hosts more than 1,200,000 visitors each year. AAA states it is the most popular tourist destination in the state of Michigan. Mackinaw City is located on the Straits of Mackinac, which is also pronounced Mackinaw, at the upper tip of Michigan's Lower Peninsula. Views of the lake and the Mackinac Bridge are prevalent from almost anywhere in the village. The village and surrounding area are rich with history as well.

During the American Revolution in 1779-1781, the British dismantled the garrison at Michilimackinac (*don't worry, I couldn't pronounce it either*), and moved it and the fur trade to Mackinac Island. The steep limestone cliffs were an ideal location for a fort. As a result of the American victory in the war, the island became United States territory. In 1812, war again broke out between the United States and Great Britain. During the night, British soldiers landed on the north shore of the island, moved their artillery to high ground and prepared to attack. The American soldiers, caught unaware, surrendered without a fight. Two years later, in the only battle ever fought on the island, American soldiers attempted to recapture Fort Mackinac, but were soundly defeated.

Ah, the bridge. The Mackinac Bridge, also called the Mighty Mac, is five miles long from end to end, with a span of 3,800 feet over the Straits of Mackinac, where Lake Huron and Lake Michigan meet. It rises 55 stories above the water, and has more than 42,000 miles of wire comprising the main cables for the suspension span. The idea for a bridge to cross the Straits was conceived in the late 1800s, but it wasn't until 1950 that the Mackinac Bridge Authority was created.

Construction began in 1954 with an estimated budget of $70 million, and took 42 months to build. The bridge officially opened on November 1, 1957, at a final cost of more than $100 million, and held the record for the world's longest suspension bridge for more than 50 years. On June 25, 1998, the bridge celebrated its 100-millionth crossing. In August, when we crossed the bridge, the Bridge Authority showed almost 529,000 vehicles had crossed the bridge, with toll revenue of $2.4 million. Current fare to cross the bridge for a passenger vehicle is $4.

Just after the Mackinac Bridge

Leaving the village, we merged onto Interstate 75, paid our toll, and began to cross the bridge. Amazing. Even though they were doing some maintenance work on the span itself, the views were incredible. Traffic was moving at a reasonable pace, and there was just enough of a breeze through the straits that the high-80-degree temperature was very comfortable.

Once we crossed the bridge, we had to stop at the sign that says "Welcome to Michigan's Upper Peninsula," and get some photos. The town of St. Ignace, pronounced "ig-ness," sits at the northern end of the bridge, and we had thought about grabbing a motel there for the night. Of course, being on the water, with every hotel in town situated with a view of the water and bridge, prices were not going to be reasonable. We were fortunate to find a

Super 8 Motel with a room under $90, which was OK, given the resort area we were in.

The usual routine ensued once we checked in— unload the bikes, turn on the AC, wash the grime and dirt off our faces, and have a drink to celebrate an amazing, albeit uneventful, day's ride.

Dinner that night was from a little café-convenience store across the highway called Patty's Pasties. (*I know, we chuckled about the same thing too...see? We are all 12 years old...*) Not pasties as in the single mom dancing on a stage, but pasties, as in "pass-tees," a small turnover-type thing filled with meat and veggies in a pie crust. They were pretty good, and just enough to hit the spot after that 83-pound omelet at lunch time.

CHAPTER NINE

GO WEST, YOUNG MAN

August 5-6

US Highway 2 was now our way home. Starting in the Upper Peninsula (*known locally as the U.P.)* at St. Ignace, US 2 goes all the way to merge with Interstate 5 in Washington State north of Seattle. We hit the road under light gray skies and chilly temperatures, and headed toward Ironwood, about 320 miles away.

This was one of the few places where we actually made a reservation, as the many hotels and inns along the U.P. were resorts, which meant they cost too much for cheap bastards like us. Again, this was an amazing ride. We skirted along the northern shore of Lake Michigan, and rode through portions of the Sault Ste. Marie State Forest, past Milakokia Lake, Cedar Lake, Gulliver Lake, the Shingleton State Forest, even part of Green Bay. And that was just the first 150 miles of the ride.

A bunch of scenic turnoffs and roadside viewpoints dotted the entire route, as well as a few small towns. Once we reached Escanaba, we turned inland away from the lake, and went through farmland and more state forest areas as we headed to Ironwood.

At one point, Mike suddenly pulled over at the intersection of US 2 and Michigan Highway 77 (*near Blaney Park*) and got off his bike. I pulled up behind him, and found out why. His bike had just turned 100,000 miles on the odometer. Yes, we took a picture of it.

Back on the road, I noticed I had a check engine light coming on when I would throttle up. Also, the cruise control wouldn't always set, and the light would come on for no reason. Plus, the bike was not running as smoothly as normal. We got into a small town after awhile, and we pulled into a parking lot so I could check some things out. I was able to pull some trouble codes out of the bike, and knew what one of them was, but not the other.

The Harley-Davidson dealer directory that we were packing with us told us the nearest dealer was in Marquette, roughly 90 miles away. I called Bald Eagle Harley-Davidson, and spoke with Adam in the service department. I gave him a quick explanation of what the symptoms were, and asked if he could look up the unknown code for me. Quick as a flash, he called back with the answer. He had found it was related to battery voltage. I checked the bike out, and found my negative battery cable was slightly loose. So I got a small turn on the cable, cleared the codes, and reassembled the bike.

And away we went. We found a small café on the side of the road just coming into Crystal Falls, and stopped for a bite. Refreshed and ready to roll, we cruised east on US 2 toward our destination, until we came to Iron River, or, more importantly, the stoplight in Iron River. Since there was virtually no traffic, and no stops along that stretch of road, I had been cruising along, 60 miles an hour, in fifth gear, with my feet up on the highway pegs. When I went to downshift to slow for the red light, however, I discovered that my shifter had disappeared. Not just the shifter peg, but the entire shifter arm.

I couldn't shift. I pulled in the clutch, and came to a stop next to Mike. After telling him what had happened, I got the bike off to the shoulder, and took a look. Again, so much for Knoxville Harley checking all the fasteners during our service. Turds. Fortunately, we were next to an empty parking lot, and the only thing separating the parking lot from the narrow shoulder of the road was a grass strip about fifteen feet wide. We got the bike pushed over to the parking lot, and Mike said he would go back and try to find my shifter. I told him not to bother.

Here's the weird thing: I had an extra in my saddlebag.

Now, I'm not sure why I packed one, other than I have had them come loose and strip out before. For some reason, somewhere along the line, I had put an extra one in my saddlebag, and had never taken it out. When I packed for the trip I found it, started to take it out, but thought, "It doesn't take up much room, I'll just leave it." God works in mysterious ways.

Road Surgery on my bike

Outside Iron River, Wisconsin

Five minutes later, we were sailing down the road once again, and came to Ironwood, near the state line with Wisconsin. We found our digs for the night, a nice family-owned motel called the Budget Host Inn. And, even though we could not get a ground-floor room, we had one directly above our parked bikes. With the temperature in the mid-80s, we each took a shower and got the grime off, then discovered the AC was not working.

157

The desk clerk came up and said it had just iced up and told us to turn it off for about 45 minutes or so, and then turn it back on. I ran next door to the auto parts store to buy a light bulb, as I had noticed my low beam had burned out during the ride, so I got that swapped out. Back in the room, we tried the AC again, and it was not putting out any cool air at all. Mike called the desk clerk again and let him know. He said that he could give us another room.

Mike asked if he just had a fan or something to get the air moving. We had already unpacked, used towels, and such, and didn't see the need for a new room. He assured us it was no problem to give us another room, but we won out, and he located a tabletop fan that he gave us. This was a super-nice guy running the place. I'm not sure if he was the owner, or just an employee, but it was nice to see someone who would go the extra mile for us over something as small as an inoperative AC.

We were up early the next morning, and ready to hit the road. We hit the requisite Mickey D's for breakfast about 6:00 a.m., filled the tanks, and off we went. This town's Mickey D's was different. Those who are old enough will remember that McDonald's used to be in small buildings, with a small dining area, and two huge golden arches on either side of the building. I remember them that way as I was growing up. The only one I was aware of still being around was in Portland, Oregon, and it was used as a museum of sorts. But, Ironwood had this one...totally retro.

Our plans were to clock about 300 miles rolling through Wisconsin and into Minnesota. It was a bit chilly in the early morning ride, and about 75 miles or so down the road, we decided to stop for hot chocolate—I don't do coffee—and we rolled into the Town of Iron River. Yes, another one. There really is an Iron River in Michigan, and one in Wisconsin, and both are along US 2. Anyway, we stopped at this little café, had our drinks, and we were westbound once again.

About five miles later, my check engine light came on again. We pulled over, checked the codes again, and found the same battery voltage code. Again. I pulled the seat, checked the battery connections, put the seat back on, checked the connection at the voltage regulator, cleared the codes, and started the bike. No light. Yay. And away we went...for about 25 miles until the light popped back on.

By this time, I knew I had a charging system or battery failure, and we decided to blast our way into Duluth—which was roughly twenty miles away at this point—to hit the Harley dealer to get it checked out. The dealer directory gave us the address and, after a few U-turns and illegal turns, we rolled into Harley-Davidson Sport Center in Duluth at 9:15, just after they opened.

I rolled back to the service department, and told the guy at the desk my situation: I was traveling, a long way from home, the check engine light is on with battery voltage codes, and I suspected I had a bad stator. Could they check it out for me?

At this point, let me give you a little background. Harley dealers, in general, will pretty much drop everything to get a traveler into the shop. I worked at a dealer for quite a few years, and we always made room for travelers. If we had to push a scheduled bike back a bit to accommodate the traveler, we did, and never had a complaint from the scheduled customer. Sometimes, all we could do is a diagnosis, sometimes a repair would take all day, but we would do what we could.

Obviously these guys didn't feel the same way. Jerks.

The guy said, without looking up from his desk, "I'm busy. I can't touch it till Tuesday."

Really. I reiterated that I was traveling, and virtually stranded, as there was mostly remote country west of there.

"Nope," he said, "can't help ya. Probably don't have a stator in stock anyway."

I guess he wasn't a total ass, because he did refer us to an independent shop back across the bridge in Superior, Wisconsin, called Color and Chrome.

Before we left, I went up to the sales floor to look for a general manager or someone who looked like he might be in charge and who would actually give a shit about their customers, but that was also an exercise in futility. Oh, well.

I called the independent shop, and the guy on the phone said to bring it over, and they would check it out. Back to Wisconsin we went, and found the shop with no trouble at all. It was not a great-looking shop, one of those old-school biker shops in an industrial area, filled with old bikes, bike parts and a hot rod or two.

Terry, the owner, and Mike, the shop foreman, were very friendly. They rolled my bike onto a rack, and had one of their guys check it out. Sure enough, the stator, which is like an alternator, was dead. That usually means the voltage regulator is dead too. Fortunately, they located the needed parts—at the Harley dealer that "probably" didn't have one in stock…hmmm—and headed off to pick them up.

I did notice, when the bike was on the rack, that my back tire was bald. Not slightly worn, not almost bald, but Bruce Willis bad ass bald. I told Terry to pick up a tire, and replace it too.

These guys were awesome. I coordinated everything with my extended warranty company for them, since they didn't normally deal with that kind of stuff. They got my scoot repaired, put a new tire on, and we were ready to roll.

What I came to find out while the tech (*another Mike*) was working on my bike was that they had called him in on his day off to get me back on the road. Terry knows how to run a shop, and even more important, knows the meaning and value of customer service.

While we were waiting for the repairs to get done, I called Knoxville Harley-Davidson and spoke with the general manager, DJ. To put it bluntly, I was pissed. I was still pissed about the joker at the dealer in Duluth. But, more so, the whole experience from Knoxville was eating at me.

We'd had our bikes serviced on the road for a reason. We were in some pretty remote areas, we were putting a lot of miles on the bikes, and we wanted professionals to check them out.

After Mike's two incidents with loose battery cables, my loose cable, my shifter falling off, and a bald back tire, it was obvious to me that they basically changed the oils and sent us on our way.

I voiced my complaints to the manager, and told him his department had missed a guaranteed sale, because if they had told me my rear tire was worn out, I would have replaced it then and there. DJ said he would check into it and call me back. I figured that was the end of it. At least I felt better for bitching about it.

Surprisingly, he did call back, about ten minutes later. He apologized, stated that he had talked to his service manager, and said he really had no solid answers for me. He did say the tech said he told me about my tire. And I mentioned, again, that I was traveling, and there would have been no question that I would have replaced the tire.

He apologized again, said they wanted their customers to be happy with the services they received, and wanted to make it right. I told him there really was nothing to do. I was traveling through the area, and would likely never be back in Knoxville. Nevertheless, he offered to send me a $50 gift card good at any Harley dealer as a concession. Good enough. He was a very nice guy. But I still would not recommend anyone going to Knoxville H-D. I'm kind of a jerk that way.

Meanwhile, back in the shop, Mike and Terry had my scoot repaired and back on the ground by about 2:30 p.m., just in time for the thunderstorm. Yes. Big, black, rolling clouds, booming thunder, jagged lightning, and rain. I'm a sucker for thunderstorms, love them to death, and it was awesome to look at—not so much to ride in. After suiting up in our rain gear, Mike and I headed off for Duluth to find a motel for the night.

A final note on this adventure. If you are ever in the Duluth-Superior area, pop into Color and Chrome. Those guys were righteous.

As far as motels went, there weren't any. Oh, we saw a lot of hotels and motels, but no one had a vacancy. WTF? It's Duluth for God's sake. Who wants to stay in Duluth? (*sorry, Duluthians*). A clerk at a really nice Days Inn we stopped at, and dripped water all over their nice shiny floors, said they had numerous events and concerts going on that weekend, and all the hotels in town were full. Wonderful. He asked us where we were headed, and we told him we were running US 2 all the way across to Washington. He said our best bet would likely be Grand Rapids, about 90 miles away. By now it was about 3:30, and it was pouring. We had no choice, so we saddled up, kicked the bikes into gear and headed out.

On our way out of town, in the drenching rain, I pulled over in a Dairy Queen parking lot, much to Mike's dismay. The reason? My bike had just hit 100,000 miles. Of course, I had to get a picture of it.

Back on the road, we maneuvered our way out of the bustling metropolis of Duluth, and headed into the farm country of Minnesota. It actually was a nice ride and, even though the weather forecast showed rain and thunderstorms all the way across our route, about twenty miles out of town the rain let up, and by 30 miles, or so, it had stopped.

Feeling free

Between Duluth and Floodwood, Minnesota

We came into a town called Floodwood after 50 miles or so. Then, on the left, was a small eight-room motel called the Stardust...and a vacancy sign out front. Hallelujah.

We pulled in, went up to the office, and found the door was locked. A sign on the door said something to the effect of, "I'm gone, be back about 6. Call this number if you need anything." You gotta love small towns. I called the number, and the lady who answered said she did have a room for $70, including tax. I gave her my credit card number. She said she'd bring a receipt by when she got back, and that we were in Room 2. The door was unlocked, and the key was on the table. Again, you gotta love small towns.

The room was nice. It had a television, microwave, fridge, and AC, but no phone. And this place had water pressure like no other. If the shower did not wash the dirt off, it would just beat the crap out of it. Anyway, we hiked next door to the burger joint for dinner, then sat outside the room with our whiskey, and visited a bit with the people in the room next to us.

August 7

The sun was out, the thunderstorms were gone, and it was a beautiful Sunday morning. Floodwood didn't really have anywhere to grab a quick breakfast, and we somehow were not really hungry yet, so we hit the road. We figured we'd stop in Grand Rapids, about 40 miles away, for a bite.

Temperatures were mild, not cool enough for a coat, but I did use my heavy sweatshirt. After a leisurely cruise along US 2, we rolled into Grand Rapids, and looked for a McDonald's. We didn't find one. We did, however, find a little chain restaurant downtown called the Country Kitchen, and made the command decision to have a real breakfast.

They had mediocre food, undercooked eggs, tasteless bacon, OK prices, and decent service. It was nothing to write home about. After breakfast, we rode the mile or so back to US 2, and crossed a bridge over the Mississippi River, next to a paper mill. Yep, we took more pictures.

We headed west on US 2 again, and began to feel a few sprinkles. After coming around a curve, we could see a wall of water in the distance. So, it was time to don the raingear once more. As it turned out, we didn't get rained on much. It was certainly nothing like what we had in Duluth.

We stopped for gas in Bemidji, which was kind of a cool town. It sits along Lake Bemidji, which is fed by the Mississippi River. Besides, it's a fun town to say out loud: Bemidji. Yeah, I'm easily amused. Along the lakefront, they have a small park area with a huge statue of Paul Bunyan and Babe, his blue ox. So naturally we had to get pictures of that.

The rain had stopped, but was still threatening more, so we headed back out of town still wearing the raingear. Of course, ten miles down the road, the clouds disappeared, the sun came out, and the temperature went up—not drastically, probably into the mid-70s. But it was still warm enough that we stopped at a rest area and shed some clothing. There were a few other bikes there, and we chatted with a couple of guys on BMWs for a bit about touring, road riding, and so on.

Our stomachs were starting to make it known that lunch would be a good idea soon. So, probably an hour or so later, we found ourselves cruising through Crookston, a small town just east of the Minnesota-North Dakota border. There was a family restaurant along the main road through town called RBJ's, that looked fairly busy. It being Sunday, about noon-ish, all the church people were there eating brunch, or lunch, or whatever they eat in Minnesota. So we stopped.

This was not our day for good food.

I ordered a French dip sandwich and, unbelievably, they screwed it up. The waitress, friendly enough, but obviously not used to seeing road-worn bikers, brought our plates and disappeared. This sandwich was huge. Or, at least the bread was...I swear it was half a loaf of French bread. Instead of being piled high with sliced roast beef, it had four small chunks of beef, like pot roast. That's it. I was going to say something, but by then we were starving, the restaurant was very busy, and we could not find our waitress. I wolfed it down, ate the fries, drank my Coke, and we got the hell out of there.

We made the easy ride across the state line into North Dakota and Grand Forks. We stopped at a truck stop to use their wi-fi, and grabbed the laptop to find a motel. There were a few in the immediate vicinity, so we gassed up and headed off to look for a room.

There weren't any. Just like Duluth, every hotel and motel in town was full. OK, it was Sunday, and it was North Dakota. What the hell? The third motel we checked finally told us why. The motels were all booked mainly because of the oil boom going on, and all the oil field workers were staying in town. But it was also because the local flour mill workers were on strike. The company brought in temporary workers, and was putting them up in the hotels as well.

Grand Forks is not a small town. The 2011 census shows a population of more than 52,000 people. It has a varied employment base, including the largest flour mill in the United States, North Dakota Mill and Elevator; Grand Forks Air Force Base; wind turbine manufacturer LM Glasfiber; potato processor JR Simplot; and the University of North Dakota.

And yet, every hotel was booked. So we asked the logical question: How far was it to the next town with a motel? That would be Devil's Lake, a mere 90 miles away, across nothing but prairie and scrubland.

So, away we rode, westbound for Devil's Lake. This part of North Dakota really has nothing in the way of scenery (*wait, doesn't that pretty much describe ALL of NoDak?*), so we twisted up the throttles and sailed at a leisurely 80 miles an hour along the highway. We made it into Devil's Lake, and the first few hotels and motels we came across had the dreaded "No Vacancy" sign out. Damn.

Welcome to North Dakota. Our first impression of Devils' Lake was that it was just a weird, dirty little town, with a huge lake next to it. This huge lake is the largest natural body of water in North Dakota, encompassing 3,800 square miles in the Devil's Lake Basin. The town of

Devil's Lake is home to just over 7,000 people and was built in 1882.

We did find a Super 8 that had a room, way too expensive for what it was—but what the hell. It was kind of the "man dying of thirst in the desert" scenario. Rooms were hard to come by, the innkeepers knew it, and charged accordingly. Believe me, it wasn't a hole, but we could tell it was old, and had not been updated or remodeled in a long time. The hallways smelled of curried chicken and cigarettes. To the owner's credit, it was clean, and had a free breakfast in the morning.

A local pizza joint had an advertisement in the room for free delivery, so we called. No delivery that day. The guy called in sick. Since it was only a couple of blocks away, we decided to ride over and eat there. It was a nice place, clean and had good food. It was tasty pizza, and they had a killer salad bar.

August 8

We gassed up, and eagerly left Devil's Lake in the dust. We wore coats, chaps, and medium weight gloves under grey skies, and because of the chilly temps. That's how we started our day, blasting out of Devil's Lake, westbound toward Minot. The sun burned through some of the clouds soon enough, but the temperature took a while to climb. We sailed along US 2 with almost no traffic around us, and the further west we rode, the more I noticed standing water in the fields, and along the shoulder of the road.

At first, I really did not think much of it, but once my brain actually registered it, I also noticed the road was bone dry. Even though there were clouds overhead, it had not rained recently. About 60 miles out of Devil's Lake, we came to a city called Rugby. Since we were blissfully sailing along at about 70 miles an hour, we had to turn around and go back to the "Rugby" sign for a picture.

Why, you ask? Because, the sign said, "Welcome to Rugby. Geographical Center of North America." Really. City is a subjective term, I suppose, because Rugby is home to only about 2,900 people, and serves as the county seat of Pierce County, North Dakota. Founded in 1886 at a junction of the Great Northern Railway, it was originally named Rugby Junction. The city erected a fifteen-foot-tall obelisk marking the "geographical center" in 1931, which was moved to a slightly different location in the early 1970s. The US Geographical Survey says Rugby itself is actually about fifteen miles from the real geographical center.

We shot a couple of pictures and headed off again toward Minot. We wanted to stop at the Harley dealer there to grab a couple of souvenirs, and maybe ask about getting our bikes washed. Many dealers are happy to accommodate travelers this way.

So we took an exit off the highway that should have led us into town. It did, right into the neighborhoods and business areas of Minot. Again, I began to notice our surroundings. It was not the nicest part of town, and my first impression was that we must be in the area of town most people would call depressed—vacant buildings, run-down houses and businesses, and garbage and debris piled up in yards and parking lots.

Around a curve, we saw what had once been a motel. It was hollowed out, with no windows or doors. It had a construction fence around the property, and workers on site. The next curve put us in a neighborhood with similar sights—rundown homes stripped of their windows and doors, with huge piles of trash, and old furniture and appliances in front. Then I saw the trucks. Remediation, asbestos removal, water damage, Red Cross, and so on. That's when I realized (*yes, I'm a little slow*) that we were in the flood zone.

Let me explain: In 2011, the Souris River Valley was hit with a number of occurrences that caused a rise in the water level, primarily starting with heavy late-summer and fall rainfall in Saskatchewan, just north of the border. Because of the heavy rainfall, the Saskatchewan Water Authority started winter releases from Rafferty Reservoir on January 10, a first for the area. They cited the necessity for this as spring flood protection.

Water releases from Lake Darling, north of Minot, followed because of the amount of water coming down from Canada. On March 22, Minot received ten inches of snow and, a week later, the city began making plans for emergency dike construction.

The spring melt in May exceeded all projections, and were expected to go higher. The local newspaper, the Minot Daily News, reported that the Souris River was nearing uncontrolled status, in part due to the releases of water from the dams nearing 4,900 cubic feet per second.

Then the rainstorms rolled in. The National Weather Service repeated their earlier warnings for residents of the Souris River Valley to prepare for one of the lengthiest water events in history. Many life-long residents of the area stated they had never seen anything like this before. The Army Corps of Engineers and the North Dakota National Guard were called in to help, and on June 20, mandatory evacuations were ordered in Minot.

The devastation we saw as we rolled through town was incredible. Sadly, I could not grab photos of the area, as my camera battery was dead, and we really had no place to pull over and grab our big cameras. As we rolled through this ravaged area almost two months after the floods, roads were still blocked off, work vehicles and government vehicles were parked along the streets and in parking lots where there was room.

We made our way up to Roughrider Harley-Davidson, and took a break. The people there were very friendly, but because of the water shortage still going on after the flood (*seems kind of ironic, doesn't it? No water after a major flood...*), they were not washing bikes. We hung out there for about a half an hour or so, trying to get over the sights we had experienced.

Back on the road, we headed west out of Minot into some hills, and out onto the prairie fifteen miles, or so, later. Once we navigated some small curves and turns on the highway, we straightened out, and that's when the wind hit us. Coming out of the north, it was hard and gusty, and lasted almost the entire 125 miles into Williston.

Mike being friendly

Somewhere in North Dakota

The bikes were bucking the wind and, when it wasn't coming at us from the side, we were headed straight into it. My shoulders and back were killing me from fighting it. We had talked about staying there overnight but, after all we had seen, fighting the wind, and damn near getting blasted off the road by all the large oil-field trucks, we just wanted the hell out of NoDak. We stopped for gas in Williston, and discovered we had averaged about twenty miles per gallon since Minot. My scoot usually has no trouble averaging 40-plus miles per gallon. We headed for the Montana border, about twenty miles, or so, down the road.

It was weird. Once out of Williston, the wind had abated and, when we crossed the Montana State Line, there was no wind. At all. We stopped for our obligatory "Welcome to..." sign photo, and noticed a sign for a casino-restaurant-bar about 500 feet away. We had not eaten in Williston, as we were so eager to leave North Dakota. Sorry, all you North Dakotians out there. Nothing personal, but your state sucks. So we opted for lunch there. We rolled in, parked the bikes, hit the bathrooms, and went into the bar for a drink, and to see what they had on the menu.

Yeah, they didn't. "We don't have a restaurant anymore," said the bartender. *Ummm, OK.* Forget the drinks then, we're hungry. She did tell us about a little store-café place just down the road a few miles near Bainville that had really good food.

Back on the scoots, we blasted the eight miles or so to Bainville, and saw the little store. I do mean little. This place was a small convenience store, a gas pump— one—and a small café with about six tables. And, it was busy. We did find a table that was open, and had lunch. Honestly, it was a great club sandwich. It's amazing what you can find in the middle of nowhere.

We had eaten and rested some, so we headed west on US 2 for another eleven miles to Culbertson. The King's Inn, right along the highway, had rooms available, and was reasonable, so we checked in, and got unpacked. The clerk told us motels all across US 2 were hard to come by because the oil and natural gas fields were in full swing, and the crews were taking up all the rooms. Point taken. Once in our room, we dug out the maps and planned our next couple of days to see if we needed to find places and make reservations. The decision we came to was to stay in Havre, a town of about 10,000 people roughly 275 miles away.

August 9

The weather channel said the winds were pretty much gone, although in Eastern Montana they are never completely calm. We checked out of the motel in Culbertson and rode into Glasgow, about 100 miles west along US 2, and stopped for breakfast at a hotel-restaurant called the Cottonwoods Hotel. The local at the gas station said it was the best, and about the only, place for a good breakfast in town. Bacon and eggs, hash browns and toast took care of the hunger pangs.

We did have to stop about 40 miles south of Culbertson, because Mike's scoot kicked a check engine light on at him again, and that's not a good thing when you're in the middle of Montana at 7:30 in the morning. We checked, found the infamous battery voltage code had set again, so off came the seat. Yep, the battery cable had worked its way loose again. So, a quick turn of the wrench, and we were back in the wind.

The weather was nice and mild, not the mid-80s that we were riding in back east, but more like mid to high-70s, and very few clouds. Most people will tell you that the scenery in this part of Montana is nothing spectacular, but I love it. We saw farms, range land, ranches and, of course, the railroad tracks running parallel to the road. We kicked back, had our feet on the highway pegs, set our cruise control at about 65, and just rolled along.

Until the construction zone. The road was down to one lane. A flagger was alternating cars through with a pilot car. And we sat. At one point we got to the front of the line, and were waiting, and the flagger was asking about our bikes, where we were from, and such. She was a rider also, and loved hearing about our trip. Finally, the pilot car came back, and we were sailing west once again. The next place we hit was Malta, and I signaled for Mike to pull over.

No, there was nothing wrong, I just had realized that we had only another 90 miles to go before we hit Havre, and it was still only 10:30 a.m. Now, we do like to be off the road fairly early most of the time, but that would have put us in Havre at noon.

The weather was beautiful, the bikes were just humming as happy as could be, and the road was smooth. A quick look at the map, and we opted to keep rolling until Shelby, an additional 100 miles past Havre. We had made a reservation at a place in Havre, so I called and cancelled it, with no problem from the clerk. Shelby is smaller than Havre, but also sits at the junction of I-15, running from Great Falls to the Canadian border. We put the map away, kicked the bikes into gear, and we were gone.

US-2

West of Havre Montana

The ride to Shelby was so cool. There was very little traffic, no wind, mild temperatures, little towns, and great views of the prairies. We cruised through town to see what motels they had. There were a few along the US 2 and I-15 junction area, but we found one in town, up on a hill, with covered parking. It was an older motel, but it had a nice big room for a reasonable price, $70 including tax. We unpacked the bikes, cleaned the road grime from our faces, and headed back down the hill into downtown.

We had to hit the liquor store. Being a couple of damn lushes on this trip, we had managed to kill another bottle of Crown the night before, so it was time for a replacement.

From there, we headed to Ringside Ribs for dinner. It was about 4:30, and we were the only ones in the place when we walked in. The food was amazing. Portions were huge, service was top-notch, drinks were good, and the waitresses were flipping shit back at us as fast as we could dish it out. By the time we left, about an hour or better later, the place was filling up.

Back in the motel, we once again checked the map to make sure of our route, because we were headed back over the Rockies through Glacier National Park.

CHAPTER TEN

OVER THE ROCKIES

August 10

We stopped in Cut Bank, Montana, for breakfast after checking out of our motel in Shelby about 6:30 a.m. Cut Bank is roughly 25 miles out of Shelby, and we spotted a McDonald's as we were rolling through. So we stopped, being as we love us some Mickey Ds for breakfast.

And, you gotta love the customer service there. We walked up to the counter. The kid, (*who didn't look like he was old enough to cross the street by himself*) came up to the counter and just stared at us. No "Can I help you?" or "What can I get for you?" or "Kiss my ass" or anything. Just stared. Maybe he'd never seen bikers before.

Anyway, we got our grub, and hit the road, headed toward Browning. We turned north at Browning onto US 89 and up to the eastern entrance of Glacier National Park.

We had a nice easy ride navigating the twisties and turns through some forest land, and stopped at St. Mary, an unincorporated town at the park entrance.

The next 60 miles were going to take us awhile.

We headed into Glacier National Park on the Going-To-The-Sun Road, which is the only road bisecting the park. Cited as a National Historic Landmark, the road is officially 53 miles long and winds its way up and over Logan Pass, at 6,646 feet above sea level.

Conceived in 1917, construction started in 1921 on the road, and it was completed in 1932. With a final cost of $2.5 million, the road opened in 1933. Going-To-The-Sun Road is one of the hardest roads in North America to snowplow, as up to 80 feet of snow can accumulate at Logan Pass, with more snow piling up just east of the pass in a snowfield called the Big Drift. Sources have said that even using snow removal equipment that can move 4,000 tons of snow each hour, it can still take ten weeks to clear.

When we went through on August 10, 2011, the road had been open for only about three weeks. Construction is a constant on this road and, if you travel it, be prepared to spend a full day doing so. Going-To-The-Sun Road has also been featured in movies—most notably, the opening credits of "The Shining" (1980), the closing scenes of "Blade Runner" (1982), and briefly in "Forest Gump" (1994).

Mike and I each had both cameras out, and stopped way too often to grab photos. Yes, it was that breathtaking. We wound our way up to Logan Pass, and parked in the visitor center parking lot so we could grab a picture of the sign indicating the continental divide. There were a lot of people milling about, and we hung out for a short time waiting to get a shot of us next to the sign. As we waited, I noticed a small deer feeding in the grass not four feet away. He definitely had no fear of people, and was getting his photo taken more than the people by the sign.

Logan Pass

Glacier National Park, Montana

The temperature was mild, I guessed the mid-60s, even though there was still snow on the ground, and the ride was very comfortable. Of course, with the construction, the curves, and the traffic, we never got above 30 miles an hour the entire way. And, we were pulling over when we could to grab pictures. Looking back at the photos we took that day, I saw that we had shot more than 350.

As we came down off Logan Pass, we were headed toward Columbia Falls, and passed Lake McDonald, the largest lake in the park. The lake is one of the most beautiful things I have ever seen, surrounded by a deep forest that casts an amazing green hue to the water. It covers an area ten miles long and one mile wide, and is 472 feet deep. The Going-To-The-Sun Road runs along McDonald's southern shore. We spent about a half-hour there, taking photos, and just relaxing in the quiet of the lake.

We dropped down out of Glacier Park into Columbia Falls, then into Kalispell. I told Mike about a place in downtown Kalispell that we were going to have lunch at, called Moose's Saloon. A local legend since 1957, Moose's is the kind of place with sawdust on the floor, overly-salted peanuts for the asking, reasonably priced cold beer, and killer food. I had two beers, a sandwich and chips all for less than $10.

After lunch, we gassed up, and hit US 2 once again westbound out of Kalispell toward Libby, about 90 miles away. The road between Kalispell and Libby is very different than eastern Montana, mainly because there are actually trees in western Montana. Some winding curves, mountain passes and, again, very little traffic made it an easy ride.

We found a place called the Caboose Motel in Libby, a very nicely refurbished place along the highway that caters to bikers as well. Restaurants were within walking distance, a grocery store was across the street, and it offered a free breakfast in the morning. They even gave us small towels that we could wipe our bikes down with.

I highly recommend this place to anyone travelling through Libby. The prices are fair, the rooms are clean, and the towels to wipe down your bike with are a nice touch.

August 11

By our count, we had been on the road for 39 days so far.

We pulled out of Libby about 6:30 am under clear skies and cold temperatures, about 43 degrees, which warmed up some as we headed out of town. About fifteen miles west of town, we pulled off at Kootenai Falls to take a look, and grab some scenic photos.

Kootenai Falls is where the Kootenai River drops about 300 feet in elevation, and is the largest undammed falls in Montana. A swinging bridge traverses the river, leading to the far side of the river, which is prime fishing ground. The Kootenai Tribe considers the falls a sacred site, viewed as the site where tribal members can connect with spiritual forces that guide the tribe and its members.

We had left the bikes in the parking area, which is little more than a wide turnoff area next to the highway, and walked in. And walked. After about five minutes of hiking the trail, we reached the sign that told us the swinging bridge was still a quarter mile away or so. We did hike in a bit further, grabbed some pics of the river and the bridge, but at that point the bridge was still a fair distance, and we didn't feel comfortable leaving the bikes with all our gear out in plain sight on the highway. So, back up to the bikes we went.

We followed US 2 into Idaho and, as we climbed in elevation toward the Idaho state line, the temperature, which had risen slightly since leaving Libby, started to drop. By the time we hit the state line, which is also the time zone change to Pacific Time, we were freezing.

Mike and I pulled over, and added more gear. We then got back in the saddle, and rolled through Bonner's Ferry and Sandpoint on our way to Spokane. Sandpoint is surrounded by the Selkirik, Bitterroot, and Cabinet mountain ranges, as well as home to Schweitzer Ski Resort, the largest in the state. Rand McNally and USA Today named Sandpoint the "Most Beautiful Small Town" in the nation in 2011. I had been looking forward to Sandpoint, mainly because the town sits along the shores of Lake Pend Oreille, which is pronounced, "pond oray."

Lake Pend Oreille is huge, to say the least. It's 65 miles long, with a surface area of almost 150 square miles. It is also one of the deepest lakes in the United States, up to

1,150 feet in some places. At its southern edge lies Farragut State Park, formerly known as Farragut Naval Training Station.

Built in 1942 after the attack on Pearl Harbor, the base housed 55,000 people, making it the largest city in Idaho. During World War II, the station was the second largest naval training ground in the world, after Naval Station Great Lakes near Chicago. Almost 300,000 sailors did their basic training there before it was decommissioned in 1946. For a time, it was even used as a prisoner of war camp, using roughly 900 Germans as maintenance men and gardeners. Because of the depth of the lake, the acoustics are similar to the open ocean, and the Navy still tests submarine prototypes there.

Unfortunately, road construction in the area had rerouted the highway away from the lake, and views were sparse at best. We grabbed what photos we could, but nothing like what I had hoped for.

We cruised on into Spokane about 9:30 am, made a small side trip, and then made our way into Airway Heights, about six miles west of Spokane, and near Fairchild Air Force Base.

A quick early lunch stop at Zip's, a local fast-food joint, took care of our growling stomachs. And fresh gas in the tanks put us back on the road westbound.

This part of our ride struck us a weird. Airway Heights is a small city, population 6,100, along US 2, and most of what is visible along the highway is businesses, restaurants, strip malls and the like. About six miles from the burger joint, we passed under a railroad trestle and were immediately in the country. There was not really any major tapering off of the business district, just instantly into the wheat farm country that dominates eastern Washington. As we looked around us, we could see nothing but miles and miles of wheat fields and farmland.

Naturally, we did hit the obligatory summer construction and road repair, which caused us to stop and park the bikes for about twenty minutes. By now, however, it was late morning, and the temperature had climbed to a very comfortable 80 degrees, or so, and we shed some more of our gear.

Moving along, we continued our journey past miles and miles of wheat fields, with a few cattle ranches and small towns breaking up the scenery.

I love riding through this part of the state and, even though most of my friends find it mind-numbingly boring, I enjoy the solitude of the wheat fields, the rich golden color, the smells of the farms and fields as I ride by, and the peaceful feeling that washes away any stress I may have.

We decided to stop in a small town called Waterville, about 135 miles from Spokane, as a friend of a friend owned a small restaurant called the Coyote Pass Café. It's a very cool little place, with really killer homemade pie. By now, the temperature had climbed into the mid-90s, and we were grateful for the rest and a quick snack.

From Waterville, we headed back into the wheat fields for a few miles, and then the road began to curve and twist as we dropped down into the Wenatchee Valley along the Columbia River. We literally went from wheat fields, to craggy rocks and mountain-pass-type road, to Highway 97 along the river—and all in ten miles. The last leg of our trip was into Wenatchee, a city of 32,000 people, which gets almost 300 days of sunshine per year.

Our motel for the night was an Econo-Lodge, and we were able to park our bikes out front of our room. We got checked in, unpacked the bikes, grabbed a shower and downloaded our pictures from the day. I checked the mileage on my scoot and, at this point, we had ridden 9,240 miles since leaving home on July 5.

We spent the evening with our friends Mark and Kathy, who offered to have us over for dinner. What a great time. Mark came and picked us up, and Kathy had made a veritable feast for us. Plus they had some other friends over for the party. We were so thankful for their hospitality, it being the first home-cooked meal we'd had since leaving Virginia. A lot of food, booze, laughter and conversation kept the night flowing, and eventually Mark gave us a ride back to the motel.

August 12-14

The final day. Well, sort of. We got up, and loaded the bikes, then ran over to Mickey D's for breakfast. Mike headed off for home from there. My plan was to head over by the Columbia River where my girlfriend and some other friends rent a house every year for a weekend. And this just happened to be the weekend they chose.

Mike had an uneventful trip home. The ride from Wenatchee to his house in the southern part of Puget Sound was only about three and a half hours. I spent some time riding around the Wenatchee-Lake Chelan area before making my way over to my friend's house.

On Sunday, August 14, I repacked my scoot, saddled up and made the four-hour ride home with no incident. I took my time heading home, running highway 97 down to Ellensburg, and catching I-90 back across the Cascades.

CHAPTER ELEVEN

WRAP UP

What an amazing adventure. According to my odometer when I reached home, we had ridden 9,567 miles in 40 days.

I mentioned earlier that Mike had taken a laptop computer with us for two reasons. One reason is that Mike is a Facebook junkie. The second reason is so we could download the pictures we had taken. At the end of each day, we pulled the memory cards from the cameras and downloaded all the pictures we took. We got rid of the blurry ones, the ones that didn't turn out, and the "what the hell was that supposed to be?" ones.

It was a good thing we did, because between the two of us, and the four cameras we had, we still ended up with more than 3,800 pictures. Sadly, only a few of those have made it into this book.

I'm a numbers guy. Not a math whiz by any means, but I like looking at numbers and seeing what turns up. Our road trip by the numbers looked like this:

27 states, 1 Canadian province.

$3.619 a gallon was our least expensive premium fuel, in Cincinnati, Ohio.

$4.299 a gallon was our most expensive premium fuel in the US, in Eureka, California.

$5.32 a gallon was our most expensive premium fuel, in Brantford, Ontario, Canada.

$96.35 was the most expensive motel we stayed in, the Super 8, in St. Ignace, Michigan.

$39 was the least expensive motel, the Nevada Inn, in Ely, Nevada.

Tolls Paid:

Chesapeake Bay Bridge & Tunnels, Virginia: $12.

George Coleman Bridge, Route 17, Gloucester, Virginia: $.85.

Thomas Dewey Thruway, I-90, New York: $2.99.

Peace Bridge, between Buffalo, New York, and Fort Erie, Ontario: $3.

Blue Water Bridge, between Sarnia, Ontairo and Port Huron, Michigan: $3.

Mackinac Bridge, between Mackinaw City, Michigan, and St Ignace, Michigan: $3.50

Total mileage of the Blue Ridge Parkway: 470. And, yes, we rode all of it.

Number of road surgeries on the bikes: 8 (4 on Mike's, 4 on mine).

Yes, the next trip is being planned. I'm not sure when it will be, or where I will go, but the idea is there. Maybe I'll drop down through Colorado, New Mexico, Utah, and the southwestern desert. Why? Because I have never been there.

And that, really, is all the reason I need.

ABOUT BRYAN HALL

Bryan Hall, a lifelong resident of the Pacific Northwest, has motorcycles in his blood. From his first motorcycle license at age 18, obtained on a friend's Vespa Motor scooter; to his current bike, a 2006 Harley-Davidson with over 150,000 miles on the odometer, he has an almost insatiable desire to be on the road, seeing new places and experiencing all the US and Canada have to offer. Unless there is snow or ice on the ground, he is most often on two-wheels. His stories are told from a personal perspective; often funny, cynical, or opinionated; and always entertaining. He currently runs a website called "hiwayflyer.com" which chronicles many of his experiences and rides throughout the Pacific Northwest and beyond. Besides riding, he enjoys cooking; a cold microbrew, and good whiskey. He is the father of two daughters and one grand-daughter and currently lives in Tacoma, Washington.

CPSIA information can be obtained at www.ICGtesting.com
Printed in the USA
BVOW07s0443120614

356152BV00001B/1/P